50 TRAILBLAZERS of the 50 STATES

written by *HOWARD MEGDAL*

illustrated by *ABBEY LOSSING*

WIDE EYED EDITIONS

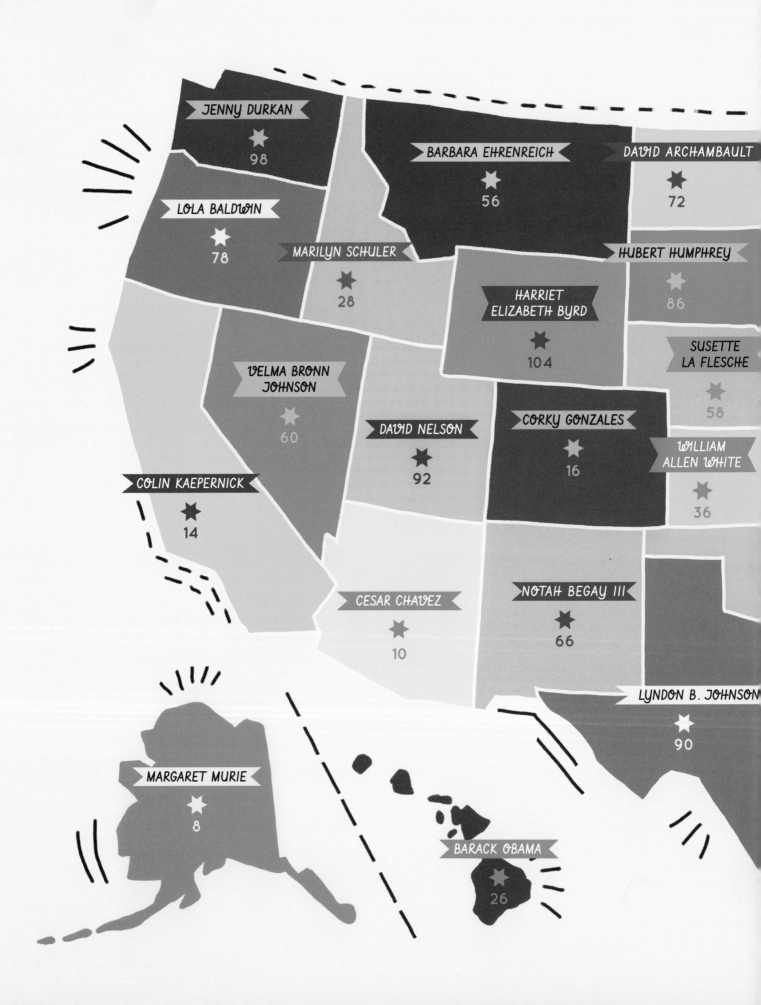

Contents

It's easy to think of history as a collection of incredible momentary breakthroughs—of civil rights leaping forward at the stroke of Lyndon B. Johnson's pen when he signed the Voting Rights Act, of women standing up for their rights through the ratification of the 19th Amendment to the United States Constitution, of Rosa Parks sitting down to stand up for what she believed.

But of course, we know this isn't true. History isn't just a whirlwind of epic and celebratory moments. Out of every corner, out of every moment in American history, we have heroes who stepped forward. Not because they saw an opportunity to make a change with the flip of a switch, but instead because they recognized that someone, somewhere, needed to start the long, hard work of repairing our world.

All across America people have looked around and realized that there's an opportunity to go out and fight to make the world a better place. Not just for themselves but for every single American, regardless of their background, bank account, sexual preference, or skin color.

THE FIGHT STILL ISN'T OVER. ALL ACROSS AMERICA PEOPLE ARE STILL TRYING TO MAKE A CHANGE. ALL OVER THIS COUNTRY THERE ARE PEOPLE COMING FORWARD TO MAKE A DIFFERENCE AND CREATING HISTORY THROUGH THEIR OWN STRUGGLES AND BATTLES.

SOMEDAY WE WILL LOOK BACK AT THESE HEROES—THE EMMA GONZÁLEZ OF THE WORLD, THE WEST VIRGINIA TEACHERS TRYING TO MAKE A CHANGE, THE FOOTBALL PLAYERS TAKING A KNEE TO FIGHT RACIAL INJUSTICE—AND KNOW THAT THEY WERE A PART OF THE PROGRESS WE WILL ALL ENJOY TOMORROW.

Rosa Parks

AFRICAN AMERICAN RIGHTS ACTIVIST

With a single bus ride, Rosa Parks served as a catalyst for change that altered the course of history. But while many stories through the years talk about Rosa as some kind of accidental activist, that isn't really true.

Rosa Parks was born Rosa McCauley on February 4, 1913. She grew up in segregated **ALABAMA**, so while her parents were both successful—her mother was a teacher, her father a carpenter—Parks saw people of color treated as if they were worth less in almost every way. **SEGREGATION** meant her schools were different from the ones white kids could attend, not as nice—and the black kids had to walk, while the white kids took the bus! To make matters worse, her school was burned down by racists—twice.

By the time she married Raymond Parks, a member of the **NAACP** (National Association for the Advancement of Colored People), in 1932, Rosa understood the need to get more involved in groups that tried to make the world a fairer place. She was elected secretary in 1943, despite facing sexism even within the NAACP, where many of the men did not think women should occupy leadership positions. And even with laws designed to keep people of color from voting, Rosa Parks **REGISTERED TO VOTE** in 1945, on her third try.

"You must never be fearful about what you are doing when it is right."

ON GUARD
FOR FULL DEMOCRACY

JOIN
N·A·A·C·P

"People always said that I didn't give up my seat because I was tired, but that isn't true. I was not tired physically, or no more tired than I usually was at the end of a working day. I was not old, although some people have an image of me as being old then. I was forty-two. No, the only tired I was, was tired of giving in."

> "I did not want to be mistreated, I did not want to be deprived of a seat that I had paid for. It was just time."

ALABAMA

NAME: Rosa Parks

TRAILBLAZER OF ACTIVISM AND HUMAN RIGHTS

BORN: 1913 **DIED:** 2005

WHY? Rosa Parks represented generations of African Americans who faced discrimination and worse in the American South. Parks and her allies reached the breaking point, and decided, through mass action, to say: enough.

Parks paid a price for it, unable to work in Alabama, she and her husband moved to **DETROIT**. There, she helped a young Congressional candidate named John Conyers get elected. Parks went on to work in his office for the next 23 years.

The President of the United States of America

Presidential Medal of Freedom

Rosa L. Parks

Then came the ride that changed everything. On December 1, 1955, Rosa Parks was riding a **MONTGOMERY, ALABAMA CITY BUS.** The law at that time said that if a white person wanted a seat, a black person had to give it up. White bus driver James Blake ordered Parks to do so. Parks **REFUSED**. What followed was an African American **BOYCOTT** of the Montgomery buses until the law changed. Parks was found guilty of disorderly conduct and fined $10. But her action touched off the collective force of a community that ultimately bent the people of Montgomery, Alabama toward an important symbol of **EQUALITY**, foreshadowing the end of segregation itself.

THE TRAILBLAZE CONTINUES... Parks died in 2005 but she has been honored many times. A street in Detroit and the library and museum at Troy University are all named after her. She received the **PRESIDENTIAL MEDAL OF FREEDOM**, and the very bus on which she made her stand is now in The Henry Ford Museum. Her papers can be found in the Library of Congress.

Margaret Murie

Long before she moved presidents, Murie graduated from Alaska Agricultural College and School of Mines, the very **FIRST WOMAN** to do so! "Mardy" married her husband, Olaus, a biologist whom she met in Fairbanks, in a ceremony as the sun rose. They traveled to the Koyukuk for their honeymoon, and enjoyed **"JOY IN COMPANIONSHIP AND IN THE SIMPLE THINGS."**

"Do I dare hope to believe that one of my great-grandchildren may someday journey to Sheenkaj and still find the gray wolf trotting across the ice of Lobo Lake?"

Known as the "Grandmother of the Conservation Movement", Murie moved to Alaska aged five, and grew up in a log cabin decades before Alaska even became a state. By the end of her life, she'd been honored by President Bill Clinton with the **MEDAL OF FREEDOM**, after convincing President Dwight D. Eisenhower to designate eight million acres as the **ARCTIC NATIONAL WILDLIFE REFUGE (ANWR)**, and decades later, President Jimmy Carter to more than double that area of **PROTECTED LAND**.

"Wilderness itself is the basis of all our civilization. I wonder if we have enough reverence for life to concede to wilderness the right to live on?"

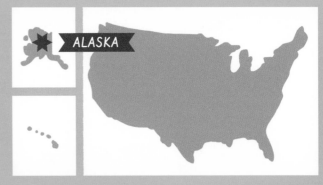

ALASKA

NAME: Margaret Murie

TRAILBLAZER OF ANIMAL ACTIVISM AND LAND RIGHTS

BORN: 1902 DIED: 2003

WHY? The twentieth century brought unprecedented growth and technology to the United States. Murie rightly feared that without a human decision to set aside some of the untouched land, we'd lose it forever. She spent the better part of that century making sure it didn't happen on her watch.

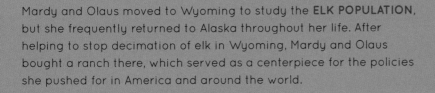

Mardy and Olaus moved to Wyoming to study the **ELK POPULATION**, but she frequently returned to Alaska throughout her life. After helping to stop decimation of elk in Wyoming, Mardy and Olaus bought a ranch there, which served as a centerpiece for the policies she pushed for in America and around the world.

THE TRAILBLAZE CONTINUES... The Murie Ranch continues to grow. It was designated a **NATIONAL HISTORIC LANDMARK** in 2006. In 2015 it became part of Teton Science Schools, geared around place-based education. And as the government threatened to bring drilling to ANWR, Alaskan voices rose in **PROTEST**. Margaret Murie's vision for the future was theirs as well.

ANWR

"I hope that the United States of America is not so rich that she can afford to let these wildernesses pass by. Or so poor that she cannot afford to keep them."

Cesar Chavez

Cesar Chavez, as much as anyone, pushed the **FAIR TREATMENT OF FARM WORKERS** forward in America, while serving as a vital example that labor rights must not be an issue for white workers alone. Born in Yuma, Arizona, one of six children, Chavez and his family moved to California after Chavez's father was cheated out of his home. His schooling ended in seventh grade, so he could **WORK FULL-TIME** and keep his mother from having to work in the fields.

By 1952, he'd joined the **COMMUNITY SERVICE ORGANIZATION**, and by 1958, he was the group's national director, working diligently to get Mexican Americans registered to vote. Then in 1962, he left the CSO to start what became the **NATIONAL FARM WORKERS ASSOCIATION**, changing the balance of power for workers forever.

"Preservation of one's own culture does not require contempt or disrespect for other cultures."

BOYCOTT LETTUCE

> *"Sometimes, fathers and mothers would take money out of their meagre food budgets just because they believed that farm workers could and must build their own union. I remember thinking then that with spirit like that... we had to win. No force on earth could stop us."*

ARIZONA

BOYCOTT LETTUCE

NFWA

BOYCOTT GRAPES

NAME: Cesar Chavez

LABOR LEADER AND CIVIL RIGHTS ACTIVIST

BORN: 1927 **DIED:** 1993

WHY? He started the National Farm Workers Association (now the United Farm Workers) who ultimately served as the bargaining organization for more than 50,000 workers in California and Florida alone by the late 1970s.

HUELGA HUELGA

BOYC LETT

USA 37

In 1970 Chavez took part in the **SALAD BOWL STRIKE** which ultimately led to higher wages for those growing lettuce. The five-year **GRAPE STRIKE** led to institutional support from Walter Reuther and even members of Congress.

THE TRAILBLAZE CONTINUES... there is a portrait of Chavez in the National Gallery in Washington, D.C., while he's also appeared on a **POSTAGE STAMP.** In 1994, a year after he died, President Clinton presented him with the **MEDAL OF FREEDOM.** And in 2016, the UFW, still going strong, won **OVERTIME PAY** for farm workers for the first time.

All-American Red Heads

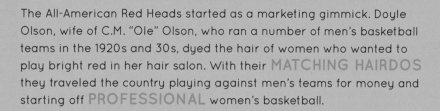

The All-American Red Heads started as a marketing gimmick. Doyle Olson, wife of C.M. "Ole" Olson, who ran a number of men's basketball teams in the 1920s and 30s, dyed the hair of women who wanted to play bright red in her hair salon. With their MATCHING HAIRDOS they traveled the country playing against men's teams for money and starting off PROFESSIONAL women's basketball.

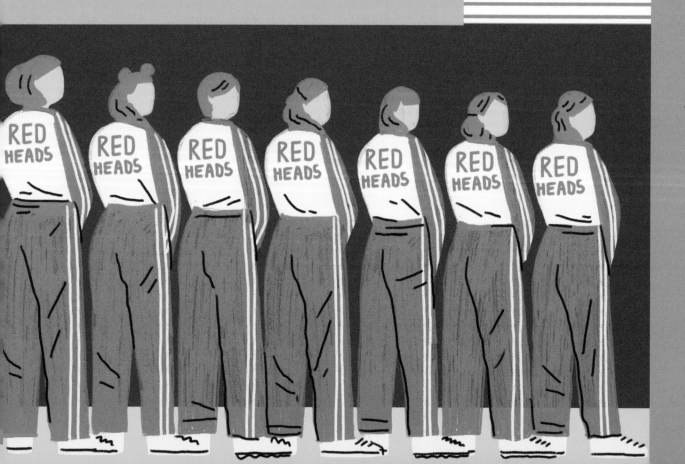

The Red Heads played all over the country, for over 50 years and multiple generations joined up. They drove themselves around, looking for games to play in front of large crowds and **BEAT MANY MEN'S TEAMS**. Their success inspired other women to make new teams meaning women aspiring to play basketball now had the opportunity to earn a living from it. Women had been able to play the sport since shortly after men could, but it was only after the Red Heads that they were able to **MAKE MONEY** doing so.

ARKANSAS

NAME: All-American Red Heads

TRAILBLAZERS FOR WOMEN'S BASKETBALL

STARTED: 1936 **ENDED:** 1986

WHY? The Red Heads allowed women to become professional basketball players and established basketball as a career for women who had already been playing for 50 years. They were now able to earn a living from the sport.

They hired Orwell "Red" Moore as coach in 1955, who helped the team a huge amount, taking their game to another level. He also added a trick-shot halftime show from his players making them even more famous and a **MUST-SEE TEAM**.

THE TRAILBLAZE CONTINUES... Women's basketball is now the most established professional women's sport. The **WNBA** is in its 23rd Season, more than 1.5 million people attended a game in 2017 and it's also broadcast on TV. The stars of women's basketball are internationally famous and very successful.

"Every day you wake up, it is Christmas"

Gail Marks, member of the All American Red Heads

By the 1970s, the Red Heads had three teams because the demand to see them was so high. They **WON 70%** of their games and were very successful.

Colin Kaepernick

Colin Kaepernick is an NFL quarterback who was willing to give up his career to bring attention to the **RACIAL INJUSTICE** of America in the twenty-first century. Kaepernick was not considered elite in high school, or later when attending Nevada, Reno, and got more attention as a baseball player.

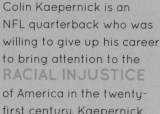

"This is for people that don't have the voice, and this is for people that are being oppressed and need to have equal opportunities to be successful."

He worked really hard to become an elite threat as both a passer and a runner. In 2011 his hard work finally paid off when the **SAN FRANCISCO 49ERS** selected him in the second round of the NFL draft. Colin went on to lead the 49ers to the 2012 season Super Bowl and the 2013 NFC Championship game. However, in August 2016, in a preseason game, he made a decision that changed the course of his career and brought to light racism in America.

During the national anthem, Kaepernick **REFUSED** to stand up and honor his country because of the **DISCRIMINATION** against Americans of color. He decided that no matter how much criticism he faced, he would not back down.

"I have to stand up for people that are oppressed. If they take football away, my endorsements from me, I know that I stood up for what is right."

NAME: Colin Kaepernick

TRAILBLAZER FOR AFRICAN AMERICAN RIGHTS

BORN: 1987

WHY? Kaepernick showed people that they should follow their beliefs and reminded America that there still isn't total equality for citizens of color.

In 2017, Kaepernick became a free agent but despite many teams needing a quarterback, no one signed him and many believe he was **BLACKBALLED** from the league. He stuck with his beliefs, refusing to **APOLOGIZE** or even promise any team interested that he wouldn't kneel before games.

He continued with his national anthem protest, kneeling in games that followed and was joined by fellow NFL players. Even women's soccer star Megan Rapinoe kneeled in support. He was called **"AN EMBARRASSMENT"** and **"A TRAITOR"** in the media.

"When there's significant change—and I feel like that flag represents what it's supposed to represent, and this country is representing people the way it's supposed to—I'll stand."

THE TRAILBLAZE CONTINUES...
Kaepernick changed the **CONVERSATION** on **HOW** to protest. The question of why quietly protesting is somehow a problem but the treatment of African Americans is not, remains unanswered. Everytime President Trump criticized NFL players for kneeling, it only served as a reminder of the problems with race the country still has, which was the very point of Kaepernick's protest in the first place.

Corky Gonzales

"The war is not in Vietnam. It's not in Korea. It's not in Cambodia. It's right here in these barrios. It's right here in our community."

Rodolfo "Corky" Gonzales was many things—a spoken word **POET** and Hall of Fame **BOXER**—and trailblazed the rights of **MEXICAN AMERICANS** in the twentieth century. He fought his way out of the Eastside Barrio, the youngest of eight children. That's where he got his nickname, "Corky"—fighting enough that he earned a reputation for **POPPING OFF LIKE A CORK**. Gonzales started as a boxer, winning 63 separate boxing matches—enough to earn him a spot in the Colorado Sports Hall of Fame. That alone would be a legacy.

"The Declaration of Independence states that we the people have the right to revolution, the right to overthrow a government that has committed abuses and seeks complete control over the people."

But Gonzales, when he retired from boxing, was just getting started. Even while he finished in the ring, he saw the huge **UNDER-REPRESENTATION** of Mexican voters in America. Leading a Mexican American contingent, or **"CHICANO"**, as they became known, he led the 1968 **PEOPLE'S MARCH ON WASHINGTON**, outlining what that path would look like: housing, education, political equality, and a seat at America's business table. He then went on to organize the **CHICANO MORATORIUM**—a march of **30,000+ ACTIVISTS** who opposed the Vietnam War in Los Angeles in 1970.

16

NAME: Rodolfo "Corky" Gonzales

TRAILBLAZER OF THE RIGHTS OF MEXICAN IMMIGRANTS IN AMERICA

BORN: 1928 **DIED:** 2005

WHY? Corky spent most of his life working on the simple idea that Mexican Americans deserved to feel and be treated as fully American without losing their Mexican identity.

Alongside his work in activism, Corky fostered a great love of poetry. He was the foremost poet of **LA GENERACION DE AZTLAN**, the generation of activists who invoked the mythical **AZTEC** homeland as a symbol of Mexican American self-determination and nationalism. Around this time, Corky created the **CRUSADE FOR JUSTICE**: a grassroots civil rights organization that hosted "liberation" conferences for youths across the nation and gave college scholarships to young Mexican Americans.

"No longer will we beg. We will demand as a right. Here we issue a declaration of rights for the Southwest, for people who shed blood and sweat to become a part of this poverty area of the Southwest."

The *Dallas Morning News* quotes Gonzales in a November 4, 1967 edition.

THE TRAILBLAZE CONTINUES... Escuela Tlatelolco, a dual language school operating under Gonzales' own principles and founded by Corky, continued in Denver until 2017, the same city where a public library is named after Gonzales. His children, including Nita (the principal at Escuela Tlatelolco) have continued the fight in his name.

Rebecca Lobo

Rebecca Lobo was born in 1973, at the same time the American law, Title IX, stating that **GIRLS RECEIVE THE SAME OPPORTUNITIES IN SPORTS** as boys in public schools, was in its infancy.

She was raised by RuthAnn Lobo, a basketball pioneer in her own right, who played when women's games were limited to **HALF COURT**. Both of her siblings played basketball too and her father was a basketball coach—playing was truly a family affair.

BASKETBALL PLAYER AND ANALYST

It wasn't long before Lobo made a name for herself on the court and she was sought-after by **ONE HUNDRED COLLEGES**. However, she chose the University of Connecticut where she led the university to its **FIRST OF ELEVEN NATIONAL TITLES**. Lobo won countless awards and trophies in her time including the Honda Sports Award for basketball and the WBCA Player of the Year award.

"There's nothing masculine about being competitive. There's nothing masculine about trying to be the best at everything you do, nor is there anything wrong with it. I don't know why a female athlete has to defend her femininity just because she chooses to play sports."

In 1995 Lobo became a member of the **U.S. TEAM** and in 1996 they took part in the Olympics where they **WON GOLD**.

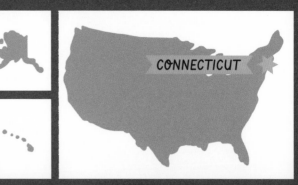

NAME: Rebecca Lobo

BASKETBALL PLAYER AND ANALYST

BORN: 1973

WHY? Rebecca Lobo's combination of basketball talent (6ft.4in. with endless array of post moves) and a savvy nature (the political science major finished with a 3.65 GPA and effortlessly handled her many media requests) made her the perfect person for the moment.

"My oldest daughter, who was four and a half, and my husband was watching UConn men...

and my daughter walked in the room and looked at the TV and said to Steve, 'Are those boys playing?' And I said, 'Yes.' And my daughter said, 'I didn't know boys played basketball.'"

THE TRAILBLAZE CONTINUES...

Rebecca Lobo maintains a strong national profile as a lead ESPN voice on women's basketball broadcasts, both college and professional. She is a touchstone for the sport, and a critical part of the story Connecticut tells, and to this day, a reminder of how every young girl can grow up to be a star on and off the court.

Lobo showed America how to be a basketball icon as one of the WNBA's first and most recognizable stars. National ads, endless news stories, and even a Barbie was modeled on her: Rebecca Lobo made sure the GENERATIONS OF YOUNG GIRLS who come after her will know EXACTLY HOW TO PICTURE THEMSELVES.

19

Joe Biden

After growing up in Scranton, PA, Biden and his family moved to Delaware, where he practiced law before entering politics in 1970. Just two years later, he was elected to the **U.S. SENATE**, becoming the sixth-youngest in American history, at **JUST 29**.

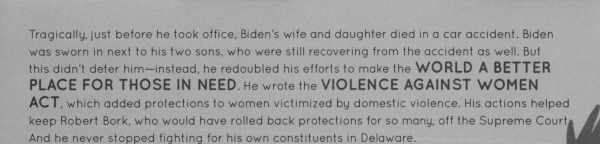

Tragically, just before he took office, Biden's wife and daughter died in a car accident. Biden was sworn in next to his two sons, who were still recovering from the accident as well. But this didn't deter him—instead, he redoubled his efforts to make the **WORLD A BETTER PLACE FOR THOSE IN NEED**. He wrote the **VIOLENCE AGAINST WOMEN ACT**, which added protections to women victimized by domestic violence. His actions helped keep Robert Bork, who would have rolled back protections for so many, off the Supreme Court. And he never stopped fighting for his own constituents in Delaware.

That work went national after he was selected by Barack Obama as the Democratic nominee for **VICE PRESIDENT** in 2008. He went on to serve two terms as a key advisor to Obama, even getting ahead of the president on the question of **MARRIAGE EQUALITY** during an interview on *Meet the Press*.

DELAWARE

NAME: Joe Biden

TRAILBLAZER OF LIBERAL RIGHTS IN POLITICS

BORN: 1942

WHY? Biden is known for key moments in the Violence Against Women Act in 1994. He also pushed Barack Obama forward on marriage equality, and provided a key voice in international and domestic affairs.

Joe Biden never stopped advocating for the **FORGOTTEN PEOPLE** he grew up with in Scranton. Biden continued to support Hillary during her campaign in 2016.

"The fabric of our complex society is woven too tightly to permit any part of it to be damaged without damaging the whole."

TOGETHER

STRONG TOGETH

STRONGER TOGETHER

THE TRAILBLAZE CONTINUES... In 2019 Biden announced his intention to run in the 2020 presidential campaign. A potential capstone on a long and determined career.

Emma González

ANTI-GUN VIOLENCE ACTIVIST

Emma González didn't choose activism. It chose her, when a man entered her **HIGH SCHOOL** and shot and killed 17 of her classmates. This had happened at many other schools over the past few decades. But González and her classmates decided the conversation that followed was going to be different this time.

MARJORY STONEMAN DOUGLAS HIGH SCHOOL

She gave an impassioned speech, one that drew **NATIONAL ATTENTION**, coverage on the television networks. She and several of her classmates showed the world that there is no minimum age for speaking out, eloquently, about the things that matter to you. She led the fight for **SAFER SCHOOLS AND STRONGER GUN LAWS**, and forced lawmakers who hadn't done this on their own to either change their ways or fumble for an answer about why they hadn't. She took on anyone and everyone on social media and braved death threats to do what was right.

She gave her famous **"WE CALL BS"** speech at a town hall with Florida's U.S. Senators. Calmly and beautifully expressing what she and her classmates wanted to every media outlet who would listen to hear.

"So we are speaking up for those who don't have anyone listening to them, for those who can't talk about it just yet, and for those who will never speak again. We are grieving, we are furious, and we are using our words fiercely and desperately because that's the only thing standing between us and this happening again."

SAVE LIVES
CONTROL GUNS

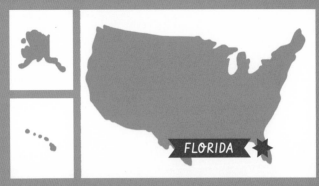

FLORIDA

NAME: Emma González

TRAILBLAZER OF ACTIVISM AND GUN CONTROL

BORN: 1999

WHY? A survivor of gun violence, has built a new pathway for gun control advocates to win support.

"In a little over six minutes, 17 of our friends were taken from us, 15 more were injured, and everyone—absolutely everyone in the Douglas community—was forever altered."

THE TRAILBLAZE CONTINUES...

Launched in June 2018, Stand with Parkland is an advocacy group that will stand alongside Moms Demand Action, Giffords, and others to work to end the horrific epidemic of gun violence in the United States.

23

Jackie Robinson

There is a reason why, when someone makes a breakthrough based on their race or gender in a new field, that person is called "The Jackie Robinson of...". In 1947 Robinson, became the **FIRST AFRICAN AMERICAN** to play since race rules had been informally enforced by Major League Baseball in the late nineteenth century. He joined an **ALL-WHITE LEAGUE**, facing anger within his own team, and abuse from many of his opponents.

He did so despite excelling in the **NEGRO LEAGUES**, serving in the **U.S. ARMED FORCES** during World War II, and continued facing these obstacles even as he honored a promise to Brooklyn Dodgers president Branch Rickey, the man who signed him, not to fight back.

And when Rickey decided it was time to **END SEGREGATION** in baseball, just after the end of World War II, his search for the right person to do it settled on Robinson. What followed was a **HALL OF FAME CAREER** on the field, even apart from his making history, a .311 lifetime batting average, 1947 Rookie of the Year, 1949 National League MVP, a key part of six NL pennant-winning teams, and a 1955 World Series champion.

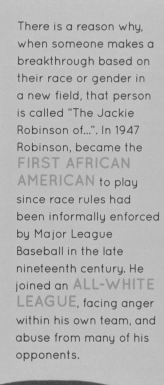

JACK ROOSEVELT ROBINSON
"JACKIE"
BROOKLYN, N.L. 1947-1956

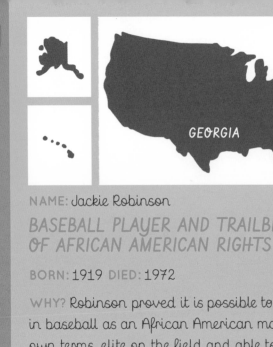

NAME: Jackie Robinson

BASEBALL PLAYER AND TRAILBLAZER OF AFRICAN AMERICAN RIGHTS

BORN: 1919 DIED: 1972

WHY? Robinson proved it is possible to succeed in baseball as an African American man on his own terms, elite on the field and able to speak his mind off it.

Days before his death, Robinson called for **AFRICAN AMERICAN MANAGERS** in baseball.

Robinson was born in Cairo, Georgia in 1919. His mother moved the family to California in the hope that they would find a better place for **RACIAL EQUALITY**. But Robinson still faced his share of racism, from boys throwing rocks at him to the town keeping many recreational activities as whites-only. He attended UCLA, starring in track and field, football, and basketball, but ultimately settled on baseball as the best way to make a living.

"A life is not important except in the impact it has on other lives"

THE TRAILBLAZE CONTINUES...
Robinson's number was retired across baseball. On April 15, every season, every single player wears 42.

Barack Obama

44TH PRESIDENT OF THE UNITED STATES

Barack Obama, the 44th president of the United States, forever changed the conversation about who Americans can ELEVATE TO THE PRESIDENCY. Obama was born in Hawaii, and raised by a single mother, only meeting his father, a man from Kenya, a few times in his life.

"My fellow Americans, we are and always will be a nation of immigrants. We were strangers once, too."

Obama graduated from Columbia University, then spent time as a community organizer in Chicago before returning to school and becoming the FIRST AFRICAN AMERICAN to edit the HARVARD LAW REVIEW. From there, his journey to the top came quickly: Illinois State Senator, then U.S. Senator in 2004, after drawing national attention with his epic speech at the Democratic National Convention.

"Change will not come if we wait for some other person or some other time. We are the ones we've been waiting for. We are the change that we seek."

And four years later, the FIRST AFRICAN AMERICAN ELECTED PRESIDENT of the United States, followed by eight years of economic recovery, expansion of health care and LGBT rights, and a national standard of what all Americans could hope to achieve.

> **"There's not a liberal America and a conservative America—there's the United States of America."**

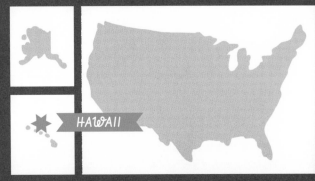

HAWAII

NAME: Barack Obama

ATTORNEY, POLITICIAN, AND FIRST AFRICAN AMERICAN ELECTED PRESIDENT OF THE UNITED STATES

BORN: 1961

WHY? Obama proved an African American could reach the highest office in America and didn't ever take no for an answer.

OBAMACARE: A two-year struggle to get the **AFFORDABLE CARE ACT** passed, which added millions of people to the health care rolls and ended the ability of insurance companies to kick a person off insurance for getting sick.

No one can ever claim Americans won't vote for an African American president, or as Obama liked to call himself,

"a skinny kid with a funny name."

THE TRAILBLAZE CONTINUES...

In 2019 two African Americans, Senator Kamala Harris and Senator Cory Booker, announced to their supporters that they were intending to run in the 2020 presidential campaign. Barack Obama's two successful runs for the White House have helped break down walls and shatter ideas that a person's race will stop them reaching this monumental goal.

Marilyn Shuler

HUMAN RIGHTS ALL-ROUNDER

In the early 1980s, with white supremacy on the rise in Idaho, Shuler put together a coalition, including Attorney General Jim Jones, to push for **LEGISLATION ON MALICIOUS HARASSMENT** to keep the Aryan Nation group from attacking minorities. The effort succeeded.

Marilyn Shuler was born in California and raised in Oregon and Utah. Her interest in human rights began with seeing her father tutor African American students in math to help them pass hiring tests. The second influence came aged 10, when she contracted **POLIO**. Her illness kept her at home for a few years and when she returned to her education, it was to a Catholic school because it was the only one with an elevator she could use. During that time, she experienced the social isolation of being **DIFFERENT** from other students—an experience that gave her a **LIFELONG EMPATHY** for others who faced discrimination.

Later, she won scholarships to go to university, and went on to receive **HONORARY DOCTORATES** from Boise State University and the University of Idaho.

> *"I think we all want to be remembered as a person that left the earth a little better than we found it ... I hope I've given more than I've taken"*

GREAT SEAL OF THE STATE ☆ OF IDAHO

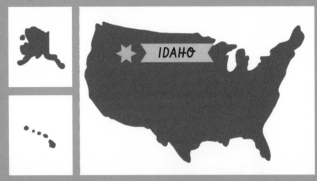

IDAHO

Later, she chaired the **IDAHO HUMAN RIGHTS COMMISSION**—the first of its kind. She also helped build the **ANNE FRANK MEMORIAL** in Boise, and supported greater funding and help for foster care, taking in children herself. In fact, she had a hand in so much of the work done in Idaho to make the state a better, more tolerant place.

NAME: Marilyn Shuler

HUMAN RIGHTS ACTIVIST

BORN: 1939 **DIED:** 2017

WHY? Marilyn was a guiding light for human rights in what was considered to be a very conservative time in American history. Today, she is still considered to be an Idaho hero.

When she died in 2017, Marilyn Shuler had done enough that she was, in the words of one of her admirers, *"a saint, and I might add, a very busy saint."*

THE TRAILBLAZE CONTINUES... The Marilyn Schuler Human Rights Initiative at Boise State University teaches students about human rights issues and advocacy, while providing community events for all.

Betty Friedan

WRITER AND FEMINIST

Betty Freidan, born Bettye Goldstein, knew from an early age that she wanted to write. She joined the **SCHOOL PAPER** at Peoria High School, but was turned down for a column, which led her to form her own **LITERARY MAGAZINE** instead. She attended Smith College, then headed to **BERKELEY**, where she **STUDIED PSYCHOLOGY**. She resumed her writing throughout the 1940s, and was a fierce advocate on **LABOR ISSUES**. However she was **FIRED** from her job writing for a newspaper covering the United Electrical Workers because she was **PREGNANT**.

She began working from home as a freelance writer for women's magazines, but she found the work unrewarding and began to consider alternative projects. This led her to start inquiring, first among her fellow college graduates, whether women were finding satisfaction in the **LIMITATIONS** of their own lives, purely **BECAUSE THEY WERE WOMEN**. All of those questions led to Betty's title, *THE FEMININE MYSTIQUE*, published in 1963 and credited with lifting feminism into the public conversation.

Drawing on her previous training in psychology, as well as history, economics, and sociology, Friedan documented the **INDEPENDENCE** enjoyed by women in the 1920s and 1930s and noted how the 1950s had marked a significant shift away from such self-determination. She described the unhappiness of suburban "housewives," who felt unrewarded by the tasks of their daily lives and guilty for not feeling more fulfilled.

"Men are not the enemy, but the fellow victims. The real enemy is women's denigration of themselves."

Women all over the world would open Friedan's book, and ask themselves:

"As she made the beds, shopped for groceries ... she was afraid to ask even of herself the silent question – 'Is this all?'"

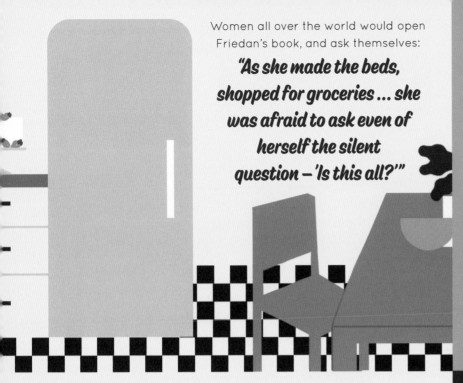

ILLINOIS

NAME: Betty Friedan

AUTHOR, FEMINIST AND ACTIVIST

BORN: 1921 DIED: 2006

WHY? Betty was a leading figure in women's rights. Her book *The Feminine Mystique* is often thought to have helped ignite the second wave of American feminism in the twentieth century.

"When she stopped conforming to the conventional picture of femininity she finally began to enjoy being a woman."

Betty's work did not stop there. In 1966, she cofounded the **NATIONAL ORGANIZATION FOR WOMEN (NOW)** to campaign for equality. In 1969 she helped launch the National Association for the Repeal of Abortion Laws, later named **NARAL PRO-CHOICE AMERICA**. Throughout the 1970s and 1980s she was an outspoken advocate for women and a leading figure of **THE FEMINIST MOVEMENT**.

THE TRAILBLAZE CONTINUES... Of all the protests against President Trump, none have had the power or gotten as much attention as the Women's March, which owes a great deal to the consciousness first raised by Friedan.

31

Eugene V. Debs

It is easy to pretend that in America there are no political prisoners, and never have been. However, Eugene V. Debs, founder of the **INDUSTRIAL WORKERS OF THE WORLD**, proves that this simply isn't true.

Debs was born in 1855 and spent much of his early life as a liberal. He helped set up the **BROTHERHOOD OF LOCOMOTIVE FIREMEN** and later became president of the **AMERICAN RAILWAY UNION** (ARU). However, he quickly found that his work with labor unions, creating simple legislations, wasn't enough to **HELP THE AMERICAN WORKER**.

WORKERS' RIGHTS ACTIVIST

"I am opposing a social order in which it is possible for one man who does absolutely nothing that is useful to amass a fortune of hundreds of millions of dollars, while millions of men and women who work all the days of their lives secure barely enough for a wretched existence."

In 1894 he helped organize an ARU **STRIKE**. Unwilling to put up with **SUB-LIVING WAGES** and **DANGEROUS WORKING CONDITIONS**, Debs and the ARU took on the most powerful transportation companies in the country. These were privately owned, wealthy groups who ultimately persuaded the federal government to intervene on their behalf. However, not before Debs had set the bar for what **FUTURE UNIONS** would demand, and ultimately, get. However, his involvement in the strike ended with him in **PRISON** and he became a staunch socialist as he completed his sentence.

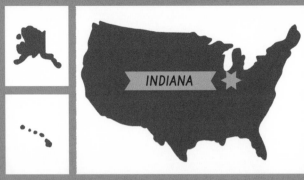

INDIANA

NAME: Eugene V. Debs

FOUNDER OF THE INDUSTRIAL WORKERS OF THE WORLD

BORN: 1855 **DIED:** 1926

WHY? Eugene Debs fought for the rights of the workers of America. He became one of the best-known socialists in the U.S.

By 1900, Debs' ability to speak to the common problems of Americans left behind by the industrialization of the country made him the Socialist Party CANDIDATE FOR PRESIDENT. He received just 0.6% of the vote in 1900. By 1912, he'd increased that by a factor of 10, getting 6%, more than a quarter of the total earned by incumbent president, William Howard Taft.

He never stopped speaking out against injustice, and it cost him his freedom a second time, when he was PROSECUTED FOR A SPEECH denouncing American participation in World War I. In front of a crowd in Canton, Ohio on June 16, 1918, Debs PROTESTED U.S. INVOLVEMENT IN WORLD WAR I, as part of a speech declaring socialism would ultimately prevail. He was charged under the "Espionage Act", a deeply immoral law that would be repealed just a few years later, that attempted to criminalize speaking out against war.

He served several years in prison before President Warren G. Harding ordered his release. However, Debs' time in prison created health problems that would ultimately lead to his death in 1926.

THE TRAILBLAZE CONTINUES... Socialism thrives in 2018, with DSA member Alexandra Ocasio-Cortez winning a U.S. House seat in New York, and the political conversation has rapidly evolved over the past few years on basics like Medicare for All and Universal Basic Income. The battles of today are those Debs would recognize, and much of the

Carrie Chapman Catt

During Carrie Chapman Catt's life America was going through a considerable amount of growth and change—and Carrie was responsible for much of it. She grew up in Charles City, Iowa, her interest in science led her to Iowa State University, where she questioned why **WOMEN WEREN'T ALLOWED TO SPEAK** at public clubs and meetings.

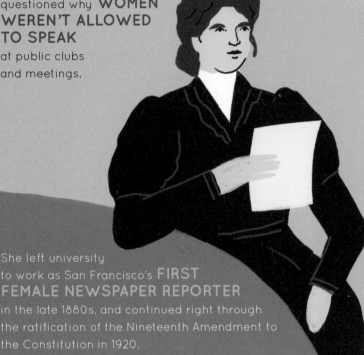

She left university to work as San Francisco's **FIRST FEMALE NEWSPAPER REPORTER** in the late 1880s, and continued right through the ratification of the Nineteenth Amendment to the Constitution in 1920.

Susan B. Anthony asked Catt to speak before Congress in 1892 on behalf of WOMEN'S SUFFRAGE. It went so well that Anthony asked her to succeed her as the head of the National American Women's Sufferage Association, the group Anthony founded.

For Carrie, this was just the beginning: she formed a group called **THE LEAGUE OF WOMEN VOTERS**, which aimed to protect women as they used their newfound rights. And she expanded her work all over the world, founding the **INTERNATIONAL WOMEN'S SUFFRAGE ALLIANCE** to bring women the vote in every country on earth.

IOWA

NAME: Carrie Chapman Catt

JOURNALIST AND SUFFRAGETTE

BORN: 1859 **DIED:** 1947

WHY? Alongside the work of Emmeline Pankhurst in the U.K., Carrie is one of the prime reasons women received the right to vote in America.

SUF FRA GE

JUS GE

"Prejudices will not melt away because the Constitution decrees equal rights."

Her work continued in a variety of ways throughout her remaining years, from protesting the way Hitler treated the Jewish people in Germany, to the peace movement, to a 1940 convening of the Women's Centennial Congress in New York, an early feminism conference. At age 88, she spoke to the United Nations as an **HONORARY VICE PRESIDENT**, urging stronger work to promote the new, fragile peace out of World War II.

CARRIE CHAPMAN CATT
JANUARY 9. 1859
MARCH 9. 1947

THE TRAILBLAZE CONTINUES... The League of Women Voters continues as a vital advocacy group ensuring all have access to our democratic process. And on November 8, 2016, as millions around the country voted for Hillary Clinton, those who knew the role she'd played in making it happen went to her grave and stuck a simple message on her headstone: I voted.

William Allen White

"Liberty is the only thing you cannot have unless you are willing to give it to others."

In 1895, he bought the **EMPORIA GAZETTE** newspaper for $3000, and over the next five decades, it was his soapbox. It was his way of making the life of his neighbors better in every way he could imagine. Seeing the Ku Klux Klan on the rise in Kansas, White ran a longshot race for governor of Kansas, exclusively centered around **OPPOSING THE KLAN**. He lost, but is widely credited with driving the Klan out of his state.

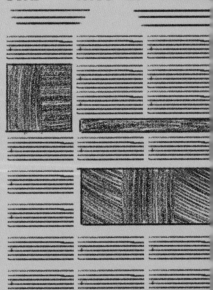

THE EMPORIA GAZETTE
THE DAWN OF PEAC

William Allen White, a lifelong resident of Kansas, understood how a small town newspaper could bring a **COMMUNITY** together and **INFORM** the nation. Born in 1868 in Emporia, White grew up reading and writing. He attended college in Kansas before joining the *Kansa City Star* straight out of school.

"I am not afraid of tomorrow, for I have seen yesterday and I love today."

THE EMPORIA GAZETTE

KANSAS

NAME: William Allen White

CRUSADING SMALL TOWN JOURNALIST

BORN: 1868 DIED: 1944

WHY? A journalist who believed that local news was national news—and just one person could affect change.

That fight took some uncommon forms: he voted Republican, even as he embraced social changes, and against Franklin Roosevelt even as he expressed support for the New Deal. Instead, he worked within the Republican Party to oppose those who believed we shouldn't HELP THOSE IN NEED, championed mom and pop stores against chains many decades before that became a common cause, and when war threatened free people around the world, he helped F.D.R. himself EDUCATE the public about why America needed to get involved.

"Peace without justice is tyranny."

White himself is the figure small town America needs today: an editor who stayed home, who built within his own community, and NEVER FORGOT THE NEEDS OF THE PEOPLE who make up so many places in this country. By the time of his death in 1944, he'd set a standard for around the country that is followed to this day.

THE TRAILBLAZE CONTINUES... White's legacy lives on. The University of Kansas' journalism department is named after him. What's more, his great-grandson owns and edits the *Emporia Gazette*, providing the same level of wisdom and continuity to a small town that White devoted his life to empowering.

Muhammad Ali

FREEDOM FIGHTER AND AFRICAN AMERICAN ACTIVIST

Muhammad Ali, born CASSIUS MARCELLUS CLAY JUNIOR, was raised in Louisville, Kentucky. As a boy, Cassius was surrounded by poverty, and more than once, his bike was stolen. The police officer on duty suggested that he learn how to protect himself—and his property—and invited him to come to the LOCAL BOXING CLASS.

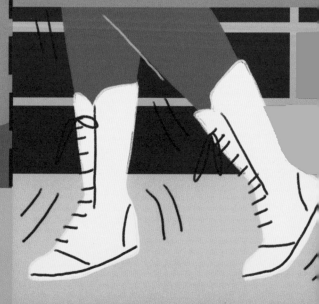

Cassius trained harder than anyone and at the age of 18, he made it to the summer OLYMPICS in Rome, where he won the gold medal in the light heavyweight division.

From there, Cassius went professional, boxing full time and running circles around his opponents. Known for being quicker than anyone in the ring, his trademark rhymes and quick feet dealt a double blow, earning him the WORLD HEAVYWEIGHT CHAMPIONSHIP three times.

> *"He who is not courageous enough to take risks will accomplish nothing in life."*

He later converted to Islam, changing his name to Muhammad Ali. When he hung up his gloves, he became a spokesperson for **CIVIL RIGHTS** and racial discrimination in America. Parkinson's Disease claimed his later years, but Ali fought on, battling to raise awareness and funds for those affected.

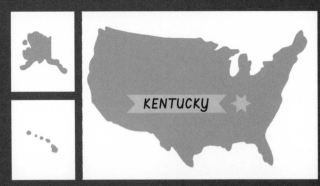

KENTUCKY

NAME: Muhammad Ali

BOXER AND CIVIL RIGHTS ACTIVIST

BORN: 1942 DIED: 2016

WHY? Ali protested all the way to the Supreme Court all the while being a heavyweight champion of the world.

"Education brings self-respect."

"Don't count the days... make the days count."

THE TRAILBLAZE CONTINUES...

Ali revolutionized the political landscape with his African American background and Islamic faith, challenging the press, who "make us [Muslims] seem like haters." Today, his charitable work continues to spread across America, from the Make-a-Wish foundation to the Special Olympics.

Norris Henderson

After a childhood of poverty, Norris Henderson entered ANGOLA PRISON in Louisiana in 1977. He spent 27 YEARS, EIGHT MONTHS AND TEN DAYS there for a crime, as Henderson explains it, he did not commit. For many, that would be where the story ends. For Henderson, it was just the beginning.

"Those who are closest to the problem are closest to the solution."

"Most people who've been incarcerated didn't know what their voting rights are. Some thought it was 10 years after they got out, some thought you had to have a pardon, others thought they had lost the right to vote completely."

LOUISIANA

While he spent that time in Angola, Henderson became a fierce advocate for his fellow prisoners. He began by advocating for an end to the overwhelming number of **LIFE SENTENCES** in the prison—more than 84% of those imprisoned. For the duration of his time in prison, Henderson never stopped shining a light on the ways those who had already lost their freedom were further subjected to **INDIGNITIES** and worse.

"You erase the years by raising the rights of the incarcerated. Prison can be a bad experience with good results. You have to find your niche. You have to be committed."

NAME: Norris Henderson

PRISONERS' RIGHTS ACTIVIST

BORN: 1950

WHY? Norris Henderson, wrongly imprisoned for 27 years, walked out of prison in 2003, a free man, and never turned his back on those who remained.

His protest over the phone company providing service to the prison led to an investigation—it turned out prisoners had been charged hundreds of thousands of dollars illegally. Finally, all his work paid off for himself, and he was **RELEASED** in 2003. The moment he left, he knew what his mission would be: to improve the lives of those who had served time.

His group, **VOICE OF THE EXPERIENCED (VOTE)** has been a tireless supporter of things ranging from **VOTING RIGHTS** to **EMPLOYMENT OPPORTUNITIES** for the people who have been written off by too many in our society. His key, central premise is to restore the basic right of a citizen to former inmates. If you've been imprisoned, you've already been punished. Moreover, his efforts to eliminate prisoner abuse, and improve the conditions of the incarcerated, continue to this day. His greatest work was evident when Louisiana Governor. John Bel Edwards signed into law a measure that restored the voting rights of convicted felons still serving probation and parole, but out of prison for five years.

THE TRAILBLAZE CONTINUES...
Henderson's next goal is to end non-unanimous jury.

41

Dorothea Dix

Dorothea knew from an early age she wanted to **EDUCATE** people. She was born in Maine, but grew up in Worcester, MA. She began to teach primary school children who couldn't afford schooling when she was just 14. Soon after, she started writing her own books.

On a trip to Europe in her 30s, she found herself among reformers in Great Britain who opened her eyes to THE NEEDS OF THE MENTALLY ILL. She understood something that we all know now, but wasn't how most people thought about it at the time: the mentally ill are sick, and need our help, not our punishment.

"There isn't a single human being who hasn't plenty to cry over, and the trick is to make the laughs outweigh the tears."

At age 40, she visited an East Cambridge jail and saw that those suffering from mental illness were imprisoned like hardened criminals. Dix worked for three years to get Massachusetts to increase the size of its facility for **TREATING PSYCHOLOGICAL DISORDERS**, then took her crusade to other states.

From Massachusetts Dix traveled to New Jersey, to North Carolina, to Pennsylvania, and more, and many mental hospitals opened in response to her work, North Carolina's even being named after her. Ultimately, 32 mental hospitals opened due to her hard work, but something more important happened: the **NATION'S PERCEPTION** of the mentally ill changed forever. By the Civil War, Dix became the Superintendent of Army of Nurses for the Union, taking her perspective on psychological care and bringing it to those most in need.

Her final years, in the 1880s, were spent in a suite built in her honor in Trenton State Hospital, a tribute to all she did.

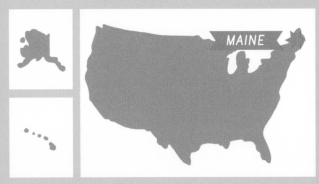

NAME: Dorothea Dix

MENTAL ILLNESS ADVOCATE AND CAMPAIGNER

BORN: 1802 DIED: 1887

WHY? Dix, a woman without a natural political power base, goes state to state and opens the government's eyes, then countries around the world, to the plight of the mentally ill.

"It's a queer thing, but imaginary troubles are harder to bear than actual ones."

THE TRAILBLAZE CONTINUES...

She is remembered in a variety of ways, from a U.S. Navy Transport ship to psychological health facilites all over the country. And the efforts by President Obama to have mental health covered in Obamacare along with physical health can be traced directly to Dix redefining mental health in this country.

Thurgood Marshall

Thurgood Marshall served as the first African American Associate Justice of the Supreme Court of the United States, during which time he fought for more than two decades **AGAINST** the rule of **SEGREGATION**.

Marshall was born and raised in Maryland. However, he was **DENIED ENTRANCE** to the University of Maryland Law School, which at the time was an all-white institution. But Marshall didn't let segregation stop him. Instead, he attended Howard University Law School, **GRADUATED FIRST IN HIS CLASS**, and set about changing the world for African Americans within the NAACP Legal Defense and Educational Fund. He rose to the level of director-counsel where, he unified the group, arguing that money needed to be moved away from funding straight African American schools and moved to fighting segregation at a higher level.

Marshall's greatest triumph was forcing the Supreme Court to acknowledge that **SEPARATE SCHOOLS** for whites and blacks was **NOT LAWFUL** under the Equal Protection Clause of the U.S. Constitution, setting into motion the biggest victories of the civil rights era. But he authored many others, from ending whites-only primaries in Texas, which excluded blacks from voting, and Chambers v. Florida, in which four black men were convicted of a crime based on confessions police got from them through illegal means.

"We will only attain freedom if we learn to appreciate what is different and muster the courage to discover what is fundamentally the same."

"Equal means getting the same thing, at the same time, and in the same place."

NAME: Thurgood Marshall

AMERICA'S FIRST BLACK SUPREME JUSTICE

BORN: 1908 **DIED:** 1993

WHY? A leading radical in political circles, he led a civil rights revolution that changed the course of twentieth century America.

MARYLAND

Marshall became the FIRST BLACK SOLICITOR GENERAL of the United States, and in 1967, the FIRST BLACK SUPREME COURT JUSTICE. President Lyndon B. Johnson nominated Marshall to the Supreme Court in 1967, saying it is "the right thing to do, the right time to do it, the right man and the right place."

Marshall had Hugo Black, a Justice who once had been in the Ku Klux Klan, administer the oath of office. Marshall remained a voice on the court for the next several decades before retiring in 1991.

"In recognizing the humanity of our fellow beings, we pay ourselves the highest tribute."

THE TRAILBLAZE CONTINUES... Marshall is a touchstone for those fighting against an unequal society. From the fight to keep voting rights for African Americans to his work against cases that allowed educational funding to tilt toward the wealthier.

W.E.B. Du Bois

AUTHOR AND CIVIL RIGHTS ACTIVIST

When W.E.B. Du Bois was born in 1868, it was at a time when the U.S. had recently fought a civil war over the question of SLAVERY.

COLORED →

By the time he died in 1963, he'd witnessed a massive civil rights era, a time of Martin Luther King, Jr., of sit-ins and voter drives, and the day after Du Bois died, the famous March on Washington took place.

Du Bois grew up in Great Barrington, Massachusetts, and said he was first exposed to RACISM when he left home to go travel in the American South. When he returned to Massachusetts, he attended Harvard University where he received multiple advanced degrees. In 1910, he went on to found the NAACP (National Association for the Advancement of Colored People) while writing and teaching.

MEMBER NAACP 1909

Then came a book that changed everything. Du Bois wrote *THE SOULS OF BLACK FOLK*, a text that forced white America to look in the mirror on issues of RACIAL INEQUALITY. It changed the way people thought of race and Du Bois became the first African American to be awarded membership to the National Institute of Arts and Letters.

THE SOULS OF BLACK FOLK

W.E.B. Du BOIS

"The problem of the twentieth century is the problem of the color line."
The Souls of Black Folk

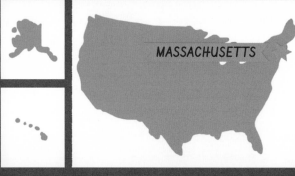

NAME: William Edward Burghardt Du Bois

AUTHOR, EDUCATOR, CIVIL RIGHTS ACTIVIST

BORN: 1868 DIED: 1963

WHY? W.E.B Du Bois' work transformed the way black citizens were seen in American society.

MASSACHUSETTS

Du Bois never saw the struggle for **RACIAL EQUALITY** as separate from the one for **ECONOMIC EQUALITY,** and championed leftist causes and candidates for decades, even running for the U.S. Senate in 1950 on the American Labor Party ticket. He provided, for those who knew of the African American struggle through Booker T. Washington, a different view. Washington largely called on African Americans to improve their circumstances themselves. Du Bois never hesitated to point out where the **SYSTEM**, and whites, were responsible and needed to do more themselves to heal our country, even moving to Ghana as explicit **REJECTION** of those failures on racial progress in the United States.

"To be a poor man is hard, but to be a poor race in a land of dollars is the very bottom of hardships."

THE TRAILBLAZE CONTINUES... Du Bois was a kind of shorthand for truth-telling on the most controversial questions of the day, writing about it all without flinching. And his prediction of how much the question of race would define the twentieth century is one of the most accurate predictions in the history of American public life.

47

Betty Ford

Betty Ford never let the constraints of her time, or what people expected of a First Lady of the United States, interfere with her **OUTSPOKEN ADVOCACY ON IMPORTANT ISSUES.** From equal rights for women to spotlighting how to best help those with addictions to alcohol or drugs, Betty Ford was going to be heard.

Betty was born in Illinois, but her family moved to Michigan, where she attended Grand Rapids High School, teaching dance to children and preparing for a life as a professional dancer. She ended up performing in Martha Graham's troupe and modeling in New York to make ends meet. Her second marriage was to **GERALD FORD** who was about to run for Congress, and it would be the partnership she enjoyed for the rest of their lives together.

Gerald Ford was a Republican congressman—because of this there were many people (Ford included) who were concerned whenever Betty spoke out. **BUT THAT DIDN'T STOP HER.** Not when she got breast cancer and spoke publicly about her decision to have her breast removed. Not when she took up the cause of the Equal Rights Amendment, which would have given women the same rights as men in the U.S. Constitution. Not when Gerald Ford became vice president. Not even when he succeeded Richard Nixon as president of the United States.

"When somebody asks you how you stand on an issue, you're very foolish if you try to beat around the bush—you just meet yourself going around the bush the other way."

Ford's Chief of Staff, Dick Cheney, asked Ford if he could get Betty to tone things down. Ford's response? "IF YOU WANT BETTY TO TONE IT DOWN, THEN YOU TELL HER."

MICHIGAN

NAME: Betty Ford

OUTSPOKEN FIRST LADY AND ADDICTION ADVOCATE

BORN: 1918 DIED: 2011

WHY? Betty Ford's unapologetic advocacy for progressive values led to great change—amongst both Democrats and Republicans. Time Magazine named her a Woman of the Year in 1975.

"I am an ordinary woman who was called onstage at an extraordinary time," she wrote in the prologue to her first autobiography. *"I was no different once I became first lady than I had been before. But through an accident of history, I had become interesting to people."*

Betty became addicted to pills and after Ford was defeated by Jimmy Carter in 1976, her addiction got worse. Finally, she got help in 1978, and by 1982, **A TREATMENT CENTER HAD OPENED IN HER NAME**, which she spent the rest of her life working on.

THE TRAILBLAZE CONTINUES...
The now-named Hazeldon Betty Ford Center has a remarkable success rate helping people overcome addiction, and remains among the most well-known facilities in the world.

Maya Moore

WNBA SUPERSTAR WHO WORKS TO MAKE AMERICA FAIRER

Maya Moore knew from an early age that she wanted to play basketball. She also knew from a pretty early age that **THE WORLD WASN'T EQUAL** for all Americans—particularly those who didn't have white skin.

Moore was a basketball wunderkind. Born in 1989 in Jefferson, Missouri, she grew up playing everywhere she could—including on a hoop her mother mounted to their apartment door. By high school, everyone understood that she was on **ANOTHER LEVEL** when it came to basketball. She won the **NATIONAL PLAYER OF THE YEAR** honors in high school, before taking home two NCAA championships at the University of Connecticut, and then going on to **WIN FOUR WNBA TITLES** with the Minnesota Lynx.

But she also learned early on in life that the criminal justice system did not treat everyone the same. She met a **WRONGFULLY CONVICTED** man named Jonathan Irons, and saw that for those without the ability to afford proper legal representation, **THE DANGERS OF "JUSTICE" WERE ENORMOUS.** Her decision to work behind the scenes on issues that mattered to her evolved into a public stance, when she and her Lynx teammates Rebekkah Brunson, Seimone Augustus, and Lindsay Whalen protested following a series of **POLICE KILLINGS** of unarmed African Americans in the summer of 2016. Wearing shirts reading **"CHANGE STARTS WITH US, JUSTICE & ACCOUNTABILITY"**, the four women held a press conference and promised to do more to bring this issue to light.

"I said how in the world does this 16-year-old get this sentencing without any physical evidence? I stepped outside of my middle-class comfort zone that I was raised in to really think, 'Oh, if I didn't have my mom, if I didn't have my family, if I was a young black man at this time growing up without a lot of money and resources, what would my life be like?'"

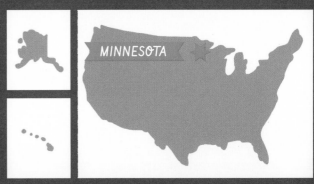

MINNESOTA

NAME: Maya Moore

WNBA SUPERSTAR WHO LED THE PUBLIC DISCUSSION OF POLICE MISCONDUCT

BORN: 1989

WHY? Maya Moore managed to forever change the way women can dream and achieve in basketball, setting a standard no one had previously met. And she's managed to marry that basketball success to her work to make America a fairer, safer country.

"I have a platform. I have a voice. I have financial means. It's contagious when one person decides to speak up for someone that doesn't have a voice. I think attacking some of the structural, systematic things in our justice system is the next level of all this momentum."

THE TRAILBLAZE CONTINUES...

Moore is active in criminal justice reform and speaks eloquently at every opportunity on issues of race, gender, and American life. She never shies away from a question and her legacy is still growing.

Myrlie Evers-Williams

Myrlie Evers-Williams was born in 1933 in Vicksburg, Mississippi. She was brought up by her grandmother and aunt, both schoolteachers, who raised her to **FIGHT INJUSTICE**. Ever since, American political life has benefited.

AFRICAN AMERICAN RIGHTS ACTIVIST

Myrlie graduated from high school in 1950, a gifted musician, and enrolled at Alcorn A&M, where she met Medgar Evers on her first day, changing the direction of her life. The two married, and she threw herself into his work. When the NAACP named Evers their Mississippi field secretary, Myrlie worked alongside him.

"I have reached a point in my life where I understand the pain and the challenges, and my attitude is one of standing up with open arms to meet them all."

"My husband, who fought the Nazis in Normandy, welcomed the day that President Kennedy made his first civil rights speech, saying the nation 'will not be fully free until all its citizens are free. ... The heart of the question is ... whether we are going to treat our fellow Americans as we want to be treated.'"

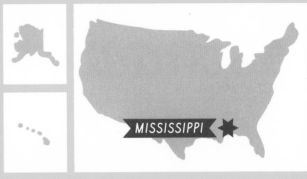

MISSISSIPPI

NAME: Myrlie Evers-Williams

AFRICAN AMERICAN RIGHTS ACTIVIST

BORN: 1933

WHY? Even after her husband was killed by white supremacists, Myrlie-Evers did not give up the fight for African Americans in the South. Her crowning moment came as she delivered the invocation at Barack Obama's second inauguration.

The fight for equality in Mississippi in the 1950s was especially hard. In so many ways, African Americans suffered in the South at that time, and their efforts spanned a huge number of areas, from **VOTING RIGHTS** to **JOB OPPORTUNITIES**, plus access to the same housing, education, and legal system as whites. Those who wanted to keep white supremacy in place reacted **VIOLENTLY**. In 1962, their home was firebombed. Then Medgar was shot and killed in 1963.

That only strengthened Myrlie's resolve. She returned to school for an advanced degree in **SOCIOLOGY**, before working to expand **EDUCATIONAL OPPORTUNITIES** at several colleges, then economic opportunities with the Board of Public Works for the city of Los Angeles. She wrote a book on her late husband's work, **FOR US, THE LIVING**, while ascending to chairperson of the NAACP's board of directors.

THE TRAILBLAZE CONTINUES... But the work simply continues in a different form, as she plans to spend her remaining years cataloguing the items and documents that make up her life's work. Myrlie continued speaking until early 2018, when she finally retired at the age of 85. The Medgar and Myrlie Evers house was named a national landmark in 2017.

Michael Harrington

Michael Harrington, despite never having experienced it himself, came to DEFINE POVERTY, its causes and its solutions, for generations of Americans. Born in St. Louis in 1928 and raised in a middle-class family, Harrington went on to attend college at Holy Cross, then studied at both the Universities of Chicago and Yale. But his true calling lay with those suffering the most dramatic effects of poverty.

AUTHOR OF *THE OTHER AMERICA*

Harrington SOUGHT TO HELP THE POOR in many ways—through editing The *Catholic Worker*, a newspaper dedicated to both Catholicism and those struggling to make ends meet. Later, Harrington moved away from religion, deciding that there was one true path to equality: SOCIALISM.

The DEMOCRATIC SOCIALISTS OF AMERICA (DSA) were founded by Harrington, with goals that appealed to a broad spectrum of Americans. The bravery of Harrington to do this, as America fought a Cold War against the Soviet Union that gave all things socialist a bad name in the eyes of many Americans, cannot be overstated.

"The Democratic Socialists envision a humane social order based on popular control of resources and production, economic planning, equitable distribution, feminism, and racial equality. I share an immediate program with liberals in this country because the best liberalism leads toward socialism. I'm a radical, but as I tell my students at Queens, I try not to soapbox. I want to be on the left wing of the possible."

MISSOURI

NAME: Michael Harrington

AUTHOR, POLITICAL ACTIVIST, FOUNDING MEMBER OF THE DEMOCRATIC SOCIALISTS OF AMERICA

BORN: 1928 DIED: 1989

WHY? Harrington was known as the "man who discovered poverty" and his work helped countless Americans facing poverty.

He wrote a book, called *THE OTHER AMERICA*, to bring to light exactly who was suffering as America saw the rich getting ever richer. John F. Kennedy read it; so did Lyndon B. Johnson. The book was published in 1962, and many of the social programs Johnson went on to pass through his **"GREAT SOCIETY"** reforms, including Medicare, owe a great deal to Harrington's work.

Harrington never stopped fighting for the poor in America, and Ted Kennedy eulogized, "Our nation is immensely richer because of his work."

Harrington's work earned him a spot on Richard Nixon's "Enemies List". Asked if this upset him, Harrington said:

"I was in good company. It would have been terrible to be left off it."

THE TRAILBLAZE CONTINUES... The DSA has never been more popular or a greater part of the Democratic party's efforts than it is today. Alexandra Ocasio-Cortez and Ilhan Omar were elected to Congress on a DSA platform. Julia Salazar won a New York State Senate seat. Across the country, DSA members are organizing around principles of equality and unabashedly calling for change to the system Harrington identified years ago as flawed for so many.

Barbara Ehrenreich

Born in Butte, Montana, Barbara Ehrenreich has informed the way people understand poverty in the United States. The daughter of two union supporters, Ehrenreich grew up understanding the **ECONOMIC STRUGGLE** of those who worked, and the way policies often made life for working families difficult. Her mother raised her to battle racial injustice, and her father taught her to appreciate the plight of workers.

"Dissent, rebellion, and all-around hell-raising remain the true duty of patriots."

"I have never seen a conflict between journalism and activism: As a journalist, I search for the truth. But as a moral person, I am also obliged to do something about it."

MONTANA

NAME: Barbara Ehrenreich

INVESTIGATIVE JOURNALIST

BORN: 1941

WHY? Ehrenreich's *Nickel and Dimed* forever changed the way we understand life for those living on minimum wage in America.

Barbara studied science in school, but by the time she had her first child, she'd decided to devote her life to **SOCIAL JUSTICE**, specifically starting with issues of **WOMEN'S HEALTH**. Horrified by her experience with the medical profession during the birth of her baby, Barbara became determined to reveal how poorly women are treated by doctors. She became a full-time writer, and her first big break came when she wrote a story for *Ms.* magazine, started by Gloria Steinem, about the myth that feminism caused heart disease.

Since then, she's written books that illustrate truths about war and peace, prosperity and poverty, feminism, and many other issues. Her best-selling book *Nickel and Dimed*, revealed how poor people need to pay more for everything—from food to housing and other items. To write the book, she went undercover, working minimum wage jobs to prove how impossible it is to get by. She has since been politically active in recent women's marches across America.

THE TRAILBLAZE CONTINUES...

Ehrenreich's latest book, *Natural Causes*, published in 2018, looks at how people are scammed by an industry based around the concept of "wellness."

Susette La Flesche

Susette La Flesche was born in 1854, and given the Native American name **"BRIGHT EYES"**. She was the daughter of Joseph La Flesche, the last chief of the **OMAHA TRIBE**. Susette lived a life of two cultures: she and her family, who were part-white, lived among the Native American Omaha Tribe. However, she and her four siblings were educated at mission schools where they received an English-language education.

Her eduction outside of her tribe did not mean that Susette would ever stop working to **IMPROVE THE LIVES** of Native Americans. In fact, it may have opened doors to her that wouldn't have been accessible to others of her race. After teaching on the Omaha reservation, she began writing about life for the Ponca tribe, which was published in the newspaper The *Omaha World-Herald* by editor Thomas Tibbles.

She also served as a **TRANSLATOR FOR CHIEF STANDING BEAR** when the tribe filed a suit against the U.S. government, for Chief Bear's wrongful arrest. The tribe won.

> *"Peaceful revolutions are slow but sure. It takes time to leaven a great unwieldy mass like this nation with the leavening ideas of justice and liberty, but the evolution is all the more certain in its results because it is so slow."*

NEBRASKA

NAME: Susette La Flesche

WRITER, ARTIST, AND NATIVE AMERICAN ACTIVIST

BORN: 1854 DIED: 1903

WHY? Susette's unique background allowed her to be a conduit for Native Americans in a critical trial that led to a judge defining them as full people under the law, with the rights to go with it.

Following that victory, La Flesche became a popular public speaker on the subject of Native American life. She toured the country, speaking, writing, and appearing with both Thomas Tibbles, who she married, and Chief Standing Bear. A national sensation, she also went to the White House to meet with President Rutherford B. Hayes. Today, Susette is acknowledged as the FIRST PUBLISHED NATIVE AMERICAN AUTHOR.

> *"The legislation of the government has been directed rather to the protection of the rights of money and property than to the best good of the citizen."*

THE TRAILBLAZE CONTINUES...

Susette was inducted into the Nebraska Hall of Fame in 1983, and the book she edited, *Ploughed Under, The Story of an Indian Chief* is still in print.

Velma Bronn Johnston

ANIMAL WELFARE ACTIVIST

Velma Bronn Johnson was born into a life that guaranteed she would understand both animals and the need to **TREAT THEM WELL**. Velma was raised on the Lazy Heart Ranch in Reno, Nevada, and learned firsthand the emotional suffering that comes with being **CONFINED** when she suffered a bout of polio at age 11.

Johnson took up work as a secretary in an insurance company, but those two lessons from childhood never left her, and one day on her way to work, she saw a truck overloaded with injured horses that someone had corralled from state lands. She worked with Nevada State Senator Walter Baring to change the laws, making it illegal to round up free-roaming horses. It was called: **THE WILD HORSE ANNIE ACT**, in honor of Velma's nickname.

"You occasionally see one, and it's the thrill of a lifetime. But mostly all you ever see is a cloud of dust after they are gone. It's their stubborn ability to survive that makes them so remarkable."

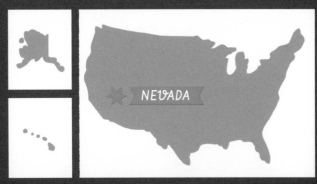

NAME: Velma Bronn Johnson

ANIMAL ACTIVIST

BORN: 1912 DIED: 1977

WHY? Velma led a campaign to stop the eradication of mustangs and free-roaming burros from public lands.

But with so many exempt from this state-based law, Velma knew she needed something bigger, and began furiously lobbying the United States Congress to do something about this. Finally, in 1971, the Wild and Free-Roaming Horse and Burros Act was SIGNED INTO LAW by President Richard Nixon. The act meant it was now illegal to capture, disturb, or injure these animals. And it was all thanks to Velma's ability to see herself in these horses.

THE TRAILBLAZE CONTINUES...

Ecosanctuaries are a huge part of the government's strategy to protect wild horses to this day. And it is the federal government's responsibility to do so, thanks to Wild Horse Annie.

Doris Haddock

Doris Haddock never let anyone tell her what to do or when to do it. Born in Laconia, New Hampshire, Doris went on to attend Emerson College. Here she met James who would become her husband of more than 70 years. The college they attended had a ban on students marrying but she married James anyway—when the school found out, she was expelled.

She and James settled down and started a family. Doris was active in several areas, from **PROTESTING NUCLEAR BOMB TESTING** to working on the **PLANNING BOARD** of the Dublin, New Hampshire town after she and James retired.

VOTE VOTE

VOTE

GO GRANNY GO

"Let us choose life and love, and happily use our selves up in loving service to one another."

But it was campaign **FINANCE REFORM** that became the great cause of her life, and late in life as well. She found herself appalled by the large sums of money being paid into **CAMPAIGNS**, when it was so desperately needed elsewhere. So, aged 90, she branded herself **"GRANNY D"** and walked across the continental United States in protest—over 3,200 miles! When she arrived at her destination in Washington, D.C., she was greeted by thousands of supporters. She was later **ARRESTED** for reading the Declaration of Independence in the Capitol building.

> *"...it is our constant intention that it should be a government of, by and for the people, not the special interests. Our right to alter our government must be used to sweep these halls clean of greedy interests so that people may use this government in service to each other's needs and to protect the condition of our earth."*

NEW HAMPSHIRE

NAME: Doris Haddock

POLITICAL ACTIVIST

BORN: 1910 **DIED:** 2010

WHY? Aged 90, Granny D walked across the country to highlight misuse of money in political campaigns. She changed the way we view political campaigns forever.

But her work did not stop there. She continued **SPEAKING OUT** and protesting our campaign finance system for the rest of her life, taking on a U.S. Senate run in New Hampshire against incumbent Judd Gregg in 2004. She also issued a statement denouncing the Citizens United Supreme Court decision—just three days before she died in 2010, age 100.

☆ FAIR ☆
ELECTIONS
for AMERICA

> *"There are two kinds of politics in the world: the politics of love and the politics of fear."*

THE TRAILBLAZE CONTINUES... Doris started a group, Open Democracy, dedicated to

Paul Robeson

NFL PLAYER AND AFRICAN AMERICAN RIGHTS ACTIVIST

American football player Paul Robeson had more talent in more areas than anyone in American history, riding athletic and artistic skills to the heights of American life, only to pay the price for standing up for what he believed in.

Robeson was raised in Princeton, New Jersey by a father who'd escaped slavery and worked as a minister. By high school, Robeson was excelling on the field: a FOUR-SPORT STAR, and on the stage, while also being incredibly strong academically and he won a FULL SCHOLARSHIP to Rutgers University. Robeson faced racism at Rutgers (where he was just the third African American to ever enroll) especially when he tried out for the football team. He not only made it on the team but also earned All-American honors, and gave a speech at his graduation URGING EQUALITY for all Americans, too.

Success came quickly in all areas—by the time he graduated from Columbia Law School, he'd also played in the NFL and appeared both off-Broadway and in a play produced in London. By 1932, he was the lead in *Show Boat*, a huge BROADWAY SUCCESS, and movie stardom followed soon after. But Robeson couldn't turn away from the racism so many Americans faced.

At the height of his popularity, Robenson used his platform to **FIGHT** fascism around the world and racism at home, showing support for minority groups in post-World War II America. This led to many cutting professional ties with him, and Robeson's income started to disappear. Only by the early 1960s did Robeson get a chance for any kind of **COMEBACK** after being blacklisted, only to see his health fail him and end his career.

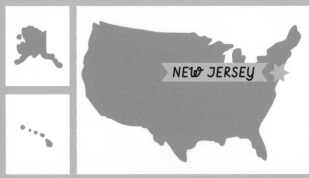

NEW JERSEY

NAME: Paul Robeson

NFL FOOTBALL PLAYER AND AFRICAN AMERICAN RIGHTS ACTIVIST

BORN: 1898 DIED: 1976

WHY? Paul was a pioneer for African American rights on and off the football field, paving the way for politically minded sportspeople of today.

"Because my father was a slave, and my people died to build this country, and I am going to stay right here and have a part of it, just like you and no Fascist-minded people will drive me from it. Is that clear?"

ACTOR & ATHLETE DENOUNCES JIM CROW

THE TRAILBLAZE CONTINUES...
Robeson's work in the public eye is memorialized forever—the College Football Hall of Fame, the Hollywood Walk of Fame, and many other honors. His refusal to play before segregated audiences helped further the civil rights battles that continue to this day.

Notah Begay III

NATIVE AMERICAN GOLFER AND RIGHTS ADVOCATE

Notah Begay III grew up LOVING GOLF. This made him different from many of his Native American peers, not just in New Mexico, but across the country. He managed to find a way on to the PGA Tour, playing professionally, and becoming a trailblazer for his people in the process.

Begay grew up in Albuquerque, New Mexico, and attended Stanford University, where he played alongside Tiger Woods and was named to three all-American teams. Together, Begay and Woods won the NATIONAL CHAMPIONSHIP in 1994, and a year later, Begay was on the professional tour.

"I'm not an activist. I'm not going to go out and raise hell and tell people that they're wrong and they need to change their beliefs. I'm an advocate—an advocate of positive American Indian issues. I just want to break down stereotypes and educate people."

This was **NO ORDINARY MOMENT.** Begay is full-blood Native American, one-half Navajo, one-quarter San Felipe and one-quarter Isleta. His grandfather, was one of the famous code talkers who helped the United States win World War II. Begay dabbed his cheeks with clay before matches, to show respect for the challenge ahead. Many observers may have been surprised to see someone with his skin color on the links. But no one could argue with his talent.

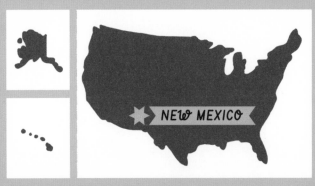

NAME: Notah Begay III

GOLFER AND NATIVE AMERICAN RIGHTS ACTIVIST

BORN: 1972

WHY? Begay used his success and power to bring the rights of Native Americans to the fore.

Begay won four different PGA Tour events, and finished as high as eighth in the PGA Championship, in 2000. He went on to represent the United States in Walker Cup and Presidents Cup championships, winning the latter in 2000. But when Begay went to Washington in 2000, he didn't use his time there to play golf. He spoke before Congress on **NATIVE AMERICAN ISSUES.**

THE TRAILBLAZE CONTINUES...
Begay is a commentator on the Golf Channel, and channels his love of golf into helping the next generation through the Notah Begay III Foundation.

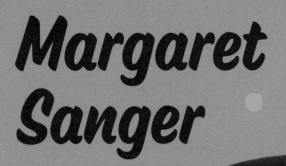

Margaret Sanger

PIONEER OF BIRTH CONTROL

Margaret Sanger forever changed the landscape of **WOMEN'S RIGHTS** in America. She grew up in Corning, New York, and after graduating from Claverack College, married an architect named William Sanger and began a life raising three children in Westchester. But a house fire sent the Sangers into New York City, where her progressive politics found a home amid the movement there in the 1910s.

Sanger's work as a nurse allowed her to understand like few others **"WHAT EVERY MOTHER SHOULD KNOW"** and **"WHAT EVERY GIRL SHOULD KNOW"**. These were also the names of her two columns in the *New York Call*, a socialist publication. A collection of those columns soon became a book, and more people started looking to Sanger for answers on things from pregnancy prevention to safer pregnancies.

"A free race cannot be born of slave mothers."

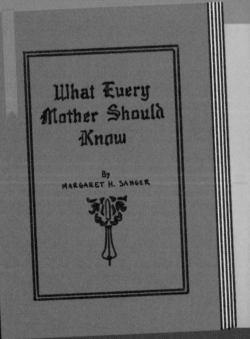

What Every Mother Should Know

By
MARGARET H. SANGER

"I glanced quickly at Mrs. Sachs... I could see stamped on her face an expression of absolute despair. We simply looked at each other, saying no word until the door had closed behind the doctor. Then she lifted her thin, blue-veined hands and clasped them beseechingly.

'He can't understand. He's only a man. But you do, don't you? Please tell me the secret, and I'll never breathe it to a soul. Please!'"

> *"When motherhood becomes the fruit of a deep yearning, not the result of ignorance or accident, its children will become the foundation of a new race."*

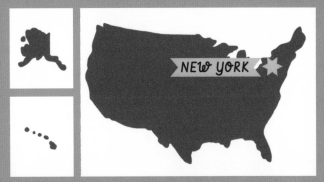

NAME: Margaret Sanger

BIRTH CONTROL ACTIVIST

BORN: 1879 **DIED:** 1966

WHY? Margaret made birth control a basic human right for the women of America—and much of the world.

By 1914, Sanger had seen too many women fall ill or die because they didn't understand the process of pregnancy, and popularized a simple, now universal term: BIRTH CONTROL. She did so in her own newspaper, *THE WOMAN REBEL*—which broke obscenity laws at the time, simply by telling women about their own bodies. She was arrested for starting a clinic to distribute contraceptives. Only after fighting her conviction on appeal was a basic right created by a judge: the right to distribute birth control, in 1918. That led to her creation of the American Birth Control League, or as it's known today: Planned Parenthood. Sanger spent the next five decades of her life working to ensure that any woman who had a baby did so because she wanted to—and knew how to avoid it if she didn't.

She retired in Arizona when she heard of the decision by the Supreme Court in Griswold v. Connecticut: to make birth control legal throughout the United States.

THE TRAILBLAZE CONTINUES...
Planned Parenthood remains the largest organization fighting the very active movement in the United States to try and control women's bodies.

Jessica McDonald

Jessica McDonald is a great soccer player—but she is also so much more than that. She's an example for every woman who wondered whether having a baby would end their athletic career.

Early in life, McDonald **EXCELLED AT SOCCER**, among other sports. Born to a family of athletes, she stood out, not only on the soccer field, but playing varsity basketball and on the track and field as well. She continued to star in both soccer and basketball in college, but once she transferred to North Carolina, it was clear soccer was her professional future.

The Chicago Red Stars of the WPS drafted her in 2010, and she played in five matches before a knee injury nearly threatened her career and cost her nearly two seasons. While she was in rehab for her knee she became pregnant with her son. Her coaches and the national press didn't believe she could continue but Jessica pushed forward with her soccer career, **TRAINING UNTIL EIGHT MONTHS PREGNANT**.

"He understands that Mommy goes and plays soccer. He understands that part of it. And we've moved around so much that whatever ball life throws at us, he manages so well."

After the birth of her son, the WPS folded, so McDonald flew halfway across the world, to **AUSTRALIA**, finding a team in Melbourne where she could **PROVE SHE COULD STILL PLAY.**

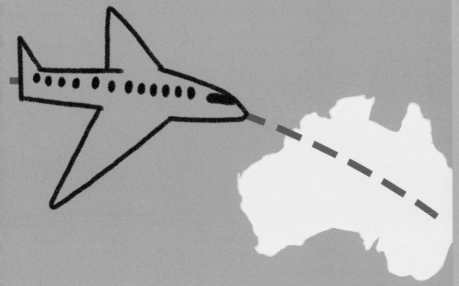

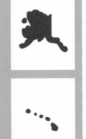

NORTH CAROLINA

NAME: Jessica McDonald

SOCCER PLAYER AND WOMEN'S RIGHTS ACTIVIST

BORN: 1988

WHY? McDonald was one of the first women in professional sport to take her fight public, believing that women can have a family and play soccer, just as men do.

A new women's league began in the United States, the National Women's Soccer League (NSWL), and McDonald came home to play, but shifted from team to team. She finally found a regular starting spot with the Western New York Flash, only to see them move to North Carolina. Still, she kept moving forward with her career, scoring four goals and helping her new team, **THE COURAGE** to get to the NWSL championship game. She even improved on that, scoring another seven goals as the Courage finally **WON THE TITLE** in 2018. In the championship game, she scored twice, while her son got to see his mom win the championship game's **MOST VALUABLE PLAYER AWARD.**

THE TRAILBLAZE CONTINUES...
McDonald is one of many mothers in the NWSL now, including national team members Amy Rodriguez and Sydney Leroux. No one questions whether it is possible to do both, and women's professional teams are working to make the challenge easier, as more of their players do it.

David Archambault II

NATIVE AMERICAN RIGHTS ACTIVIST

David Archambault II, born in Denver, Colorado, was born into the **NATIVE AMERICAN RIGHTS MOVEMENT**. His mother taught at Standing Rock Community School, located on the Standing Rock reservation in North Dakota, while his father helped establish the tribal colleges and universities movement (a group of colleges run by Native American tribes, and funded by the federal government). His uncles worked in the Native American rights movement as well.

"We are also a resilient people who have survived unspeakable hardships in the past, so we know what is at stake now. As our songs and prayers echo across the prairie, we need the public to see that in standing up for our rights, we do so on behalf of the millions of Americans who will be affected by this pipeline."

Archambault was raised on the Pine Ridge Indian Reservation, before attending Standing Rock Community college, then North Dakota State University. But he heard about a call for public service that led to his running, and winning, an election as CHAIRMAN OF THE STANDING ROCK TRIBAL COUNCIL.

Archambault welcomed President Obama to Standing Rock in 2014, and said this of him:

"Sitting Bull once asked the government in Washington to send him an honest man. If Sitting Bull were sitting here today, he'd be honored."

NORTH DAKOTA

NORTH DAKOTA

←PIPELINE

SOUTH DAKOTA

NAME: David Archambault II

NATIVE AMERICAN RIGHTS ACTIVIST

Became Chairman of the Standing Rock Tribal Council in September 2013

WHY? David's work paved the way for Americans to better understand the historical treaty rights and indigenous rights of Native American people.

He became the Chairman at a critical time for the tribe. Efforts to build the **DAKOTA ACCESS PIPELINE**, a 1,172-mile pipeline for oil, included plans to run through sacred burial grounds, not to mention putting at risk the tribe's drinking water. Archambault mobilized his people to **STOP** the pipeline, setting up encampments, protesting and getting arrested in the process. He not only energized **NATIVE AMERICAN OPPOSITION** to the pipeline, his ability to nationalize the fight led activists from all over to come to North Dakota to help. The protest worked, with President Obama **DECLINING** to grant an easement, which was a necessary step for the work to continue.

THE TRAILBLAZE CONTINUES... Archambault's work to nationalize the Standing Rock protests have elevated the continued work on behalf on Native Americans into a vital, progressive priority.

LeBron James

LeBron James already has a claim to being the best basketball player in the history of the sport. His career has seen FOUR MVPS, THREE CHAMPIONSHIPS, 14 ALL-STAR TEAMS and much more besides. And yet, even as he's worked to make himself into the transcendent player of his generation, James hasn't been content to simply let his play do the talking for him.

James started the LEBRON JAMES FAMILY FOUNDATION in 2003, right before he entered the NBA Draft. It's a common way for athletes to give back. But James' foundation has done far more than most other charitable endeavor like this. James, who has never forgotten his home town of Akron, announced that he'd be personally FUNDING THE COLLEGE EDUCATIONS of 2,300 AKRON STUDENTS. He's gone on to build an Akron public school, which means that not only will hundreds of students have access to it, but it will also be available to everyone, not just those who can afford to pay or receive financial assistance.

"Back when I was a student searching for Akron on the world map, I dreamed I would someday be in a position to give back to the community that had done so much for me. Seeing these students succeed and create a better life for themselves and their families is what drives me daily. Their dreams are my dreams. They are my purpose, and together, we can change the world."

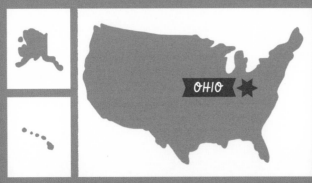

NAME: LeBron James

BASKETBALL PLAYER AND AFRICAN AMERICAN RIGHTS ACTIVIST

BORN: 1984

WHY? LeBron is prepared to put his wealth, fame, and work ethic on the line to make the lives of African Americans better nationwide—and particularly in his home town of Akron.

He hasn't limited his activism to good works using his own wealth. James hasn't hesitated to **SPEAK OUT**—against the racism of Donald Trump, about the problem of police brutality in the United States, repeatedly willing to alienate some of his fans because knew he needed speak out about what he felt was right.

"Being black in America is tough. We got a long way to go for us as a society and for us as African Americans until we feel equal in America."

He's backed political candidates as well, bundling donations for Barack Obama, and endorsing Hillary Clinton, even speaking at a rally on her behalf. Trump has attacked him by name but his work continues to speak for itself, and many others rose to defend him.

THE TRAILBLAZE CONTINUES...
James' goals for Akron: in 20 years, a meaningful change in the city's adult-literacy rates, crime rate, and its median income.

Woody Guthrie

Woody Guthrie was an instrumental singer-songwriter during a time of economic struggles. Raised in Oklahoma, Guthrie watched his family fall apart—his mother suffered from Huntington's Disease—and poor financial decisions ruined his father. Guthrie was self-taught and bright, though he never finished high school. He bought a harmonica and then taught himself how to play it. He headed to California in the 1930s, during the GREAT DEPRESSION, in search of work. Instead, he found the INSPIRATION FOR HIS MUSIC.

Guthrie partnered with Maxine "Lefty Lou" Crissman on the radio station KFVD. There he began writing and singing PROTEST SONGS, which ultimately became part of his first album, *Dust Bowl Ballads*. Guthrie then moved east in 1940, and recorded that album. That same year, in response to the song "God Bless America" by Irving Berlin, Guthrie wrote his most famous song: "THIS LAND IS YOUR LAND".

"It's a folk singer's job to comfort disturbed people and to disturb comfortable people."

FREE FOOD FOR THE UNEMPLOYED

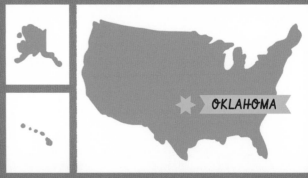

OKLAHOMA

NAME: Woody Guthrie

MUSICIAN AND ACTIVIST

BORN: 1912 DIED: 1967

WHY? An instrument of song for the struggles of his time, Guthrie inspired a generation of people to action with song.

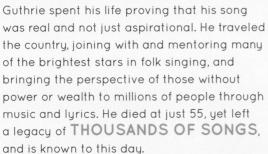

Guthrie spent his life proving that his song was real and not just aspirational. He traveled the country, joining with and mentoring many of the brightest stars in folk singing, and bringing the perspective of those without power or wealth to millions of people through music and lyrics. He died at just 55, yet left a legacy of **THOUSANDS OF SONGS**, and is known to this day.

THE TRAILBLAZE CONTINUES...
Folk music remains a means for those who wish to bring about social change to raise the consciousness of Americans, and Guthrie's brand of doing so is as relevant as ever, especially in times where so many are left behind by the American dream. Issues of economic justice, race, and immigration resonate as sharply as ever.

Lola Baldwin

Lola Baldwin proved to everyone that women were perfectly capable of doing the job she was hired to do: be an upstanding **FEMALE POLICE OFFICER** in the United States.

PIONEERING POLICE OFFICER

She grew up in Rochester, New York, before moving to Portland, Oregon with her husband and two sons. She worked as a teacher, while volunteering to work for groups that helped women in trouble. She was a logical choice for the city of Portland when, in 1905, it looked for someone to be sure the women of the city would be protected during the centennial celebrations of the Lewis and Clark Expedition. Locals were worried that people coming to the city would target and attack young girls during the celebrations. She oversaw women providing food and shelter for them away from threat and danger.

Her work continued in this vein after the exposition ended, with Baldwin working to help runaways and other people who often found themselves lost in the system.

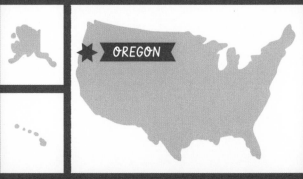

OREGON

NAME: Lola Baldwin

ONE OF AMERICA'S FIRST FEMALE POLICE OFFICERS

BORN: 1860 DIED: 1957

WHY? Baldwin proved that women were capable of being strong members of the U.S. police force at a time when it was unheard of.

The mayor, Harry Lane, decided her work was important enough that he created a **NEW WING** of the **PORTLAND POLICE FORCE**, called the **WOMEN'S AUXILIARY TO THE POLICE DEPARTMENT FOR THE PROTECTION OF GIRLS**, and put Baldwin in charge of it. Baldwin spent the next 14 years working to protect young women in Portland, while showing the public a woman in a position of law enforcement authority, something brand new in Portland and seldom seen anywhere in the country.

Baldwin was committed to her role. When a man threatened her with a gun in her own office she said,

"You can go ahead and shoot. Because my work will go on."

THE TRAILBLAZE CONTINUES...
Baldwin was honored by Portland 100 years after she received her post, with Portland Mayor Tom Potter making April 1, 2008 Lola Baldwin Centennial Day by proclamation.

Rachel Carson

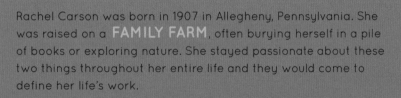

THE MOTHER OF THE ENVIRONMENTAL MOVEMENT IN AMERICA

Rachel Carson was born in 1907 in Allegheny, Pennsylvania. She was raised on a **FAMILY FARM**, often burying herself in a pile of books or exploring nature. She stayed passionate about these two things throughout her entire life and they would come to define her life's work.

She studied English and Biology, first at the Pennsylvania College for Women and then later as a graduate student at Johns Hopkins University. She earned a master's degree, and planned to continue studying, but the Great Depression forced her to find work to help her family.

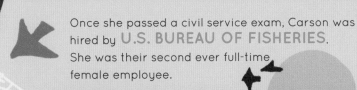

Once she passed a civil service exam, Carson was hired by **U.S. BUREAU OF FISHERIES**. She was their second ever full-time female employee.

By 1949 she had risen to the level of **EDITOR OF PUBLICATIONS**, but her writing outside of work was really starting to take off.

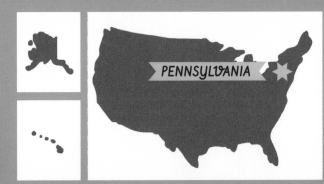

PENNSYLVANIA

NAME: Rachel Carson

ENVIRONMENTALIST, AUTHOR, CONSERVATIONIST

BORN: 1907 **DIED:** 1964

WHY? Carson was a marine biologist and conservationist. Her book *Silent Spring* helped advance the global environmental movement.

"We still talk in terms of conquest. We still haven't become mature enough to think of ourselves as only a tiny part of a vast and incredible universe. Man's attitude toward nature is today critically important simply because we have now acquired a fateful power to alter and destroy nature.

But man is a part of nature, and his war against nature is inevitably a war against himself."

In 1950, she published *THE SEA AROUND US*, a history of the ocean, which became a best seller, and was serialized by *The New Yorker*. Her success led her to leave her job and focus on writing full time, first on books about the sea, but as the decade went on, transitioning to the dangers she saw concerning **PESTICIDES**.

The **CHEMICALS** the government was using to control the pest population had horrifying effects on the environment and the people around it. In 1962, she published *SILENT SPRING*, which laid out clearly what we knew about that threat. Tragically, Carson was battling cancer throughout the publication of *Silent Spring*, which identified the many ways pesticides cause cancer in humans. She died at just 57, in 1964.

THE TRAILBLAZE CONTINUES...
No less than a cabinet-level department in the United States government exists today because of Rachel Carson's work: The Environmental Protection Agency.

Marjorie van Vliet

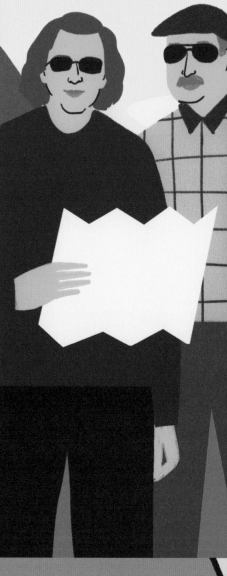

WORLD PEACE ADVOCATE

Marjorie van Vliet was born in 1923 and lived and worked as a **TEACHER** in Warwick, Rhode Island. However, she knew she wanted to make a greater impact on the world. And what better way to do that than by advocating for something big: **WORLD PEACE**.

The question was how to do it. That is when she hit upon the answer: the creation of the **WORLD FRIENDSHIP ASSOCIATION**, a group dedicated to **ENDING WAR**. But how could she draw attention to her cause? It wasn't long before she hit upon an answer for that too! She decided to **FLY TO EVERY STATE CAPITAL IN THE CONTINENTAL UNITED STATES**, and then to the **SOVIET UNION**. The latter required Soviet permission which wasn't forthcoming. The Cold War (a tense relationship between the United States and the Soviet Union) was still on going so in the meantime she concentrated her efforts on reaching all of the lower 48 capitals.

"It is tremendously exhilarating to overcome fear. In learning to fly, the more apprehensive I was before I took off, the greater the exhilaration I had when I achieved it."

A retired colonel from the U.S. Air Force, Frank Martineau, accompanied van Vliet (who had previously been afraid to fly!) on her mission. Their goal was to hit **ALL 48 CAPITALS IN TWO WEEKS.** The Soviet Union, moved by her effort, then granted her the right to fly there. However, when they had reached 47 of them, they crashed just outside of Charleston, West Virginia. Van Vliet gave her life to the cause and conquered her fear in the process.

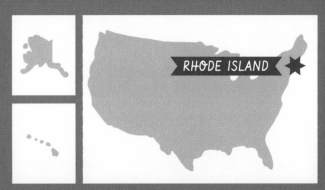

RHODE ISLAND ★

NAME: Marjorie van Vliet

ATTEMPTED TO FLY TO ALL MAINLAND STATES IN PURSUIT OF WORLD PEACE

BORN: 1923 DIED: 1990

WHY? Marjorie van Vliet set out to fly to every state in pursuit of world peace.

THE TRAILBLAZE CONTINUES...
Van Vliet was honored at the International Forest of Friendship, a memorial in Atchison, Kansas, which includes luminaries Amelia Earhart and Charles Lindbergh.

The Grimké Sisters

Sarah and Angelina Grimké, born 13 years apart, grew up in a SLAVE-OWNING FAMILY. Each of them spent their lives working tirelessly to END THIS BRUTAL PRACTICE. They also became vital voices for feminism and connected the two progressive worlds.

Sarah and Angelina were two of 13 children, born in South Carolina, raised by John Faucheraud Grimké, chief judge of the Supreme Court of South Carolina. Sarah grew up interested in law and as she got older, she started to realize and firmly believe that her family's owning of slaves, and slavery as a whole, was wrong. She ignored South Carolina law, and TAUGHT SOME OF HER FAMILY'S SLAVES TO READ.

"I appeal to you, my friends, as mothers; are you willing to enslave your children? You start back with horror and indignation at such a question. But why, if slavery is no wrong to those upon whom it is imposed?

Why, if as has often been said, slaves are happier than their masters, free from the cares and perplexities of providing for themselves and their families? Why not place your children in the way of being supported without your having the trouble to provide for them, or they for themselves?

Do you not perceive that as soon as this golden rule of action is applied to yourselves that you involuntarily shrink from the test; as soon as your actions are weighed in this balance of the sanctuary that you are found wanting?" —Angelina Grimké

Sarah also took a keen interest in her younger sister Angelina's well-being, and eventually became her godmother. Sarah and Angelina took a trip north to Philadelphia, where she encountered the **QUAKERS**, a group that contained other people who were **FIERCELY ABOLITIONIST, OR ANTI-SLAVERY.**

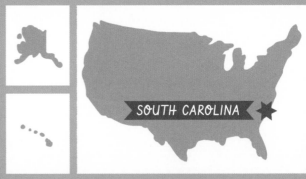

NAME: Sarah and Angelina Grimké

INFLUENTIAL WRITERS IN OPPOSITION TO SLAVERY

SARAH BORN: 1792 DIED: 1873
ANGELINA BORN: 1805 DIED: 1879

WHY? The first female American advocates to fight for abolition and women's rights.

Once both sisters moved to Philadelphia, they became more active in the abolitionist movement. Angelina wrote a letter published in *The Liberator*, an anti-slavery newspaper, calling the cause, **"WORTH DYING FOR".** The sisters represented something powerful: **SOUTHERN WOMEN CALLING ON THEIR OWN KIN** to end the hateful practice of slavery. They spoke in 67 cities around the country, **BREAKING MULTIPLE BARRIERS,** including the fact that they were women (and it would have been very unusual for women to do this at the time), speaking out on any and every topic.

Sarah and Angelina lived until 1873 and 1879, respectively, and got to see their cause, **ABOLITION OF SLAVERY,** come to fruition.

THE TRAILBLAZE CONTINUES...
The fight for the rights of African Americans, and of women to speak up on behalf of causes that matter to them, is anything but settled. The intersection between the two is a vital pathway to this day, begun in large by the work of the Grimké sisters.

Hubert Humphrey

Hubert Humphrey served the United States in several different governmental roles—MAYOR, SENATOR, AND VICE PRESIDENT. He's also the reason why the Democratic Party has been a force for civil rights, ridding the party of those who opposed the effort to BRING THE VOTE TO AFRICAN AMERICANS. His efforts led to a radical shift that remains in place today, with a major political party recognizing the need for change at last.

Humphrey was born in 1911 in Wallace, South Dakota. He attended the University of Minnesota, before going to work for his father's pharmacy. He later served in the Works Progress Administration (a vital New Deal program started by Franklin Roosevelt) and then went on to earn a master's degree. In 1944, he founded a progressive coalition called the Democratic-Farmer-Labor Party in Minnesota. By 1948, he'd been elected Mayor of Minneapolis while winning a battle over the national Democratic Party platform that changed the course of racial politics.

THE DEMOCRATS, at that time, were a COALITION of largely pro-civil rights northerners and anti-civil rights southerners. The party always worked hard to find a middle ground between them, making an effort to fix the huge problem of systemic racism. Anti-lynching laws, the end of poll taxes (requiring African Americans to pay for the right to vote) and allowing African Americans to serve in the armed forces were all vital changes Humphrey insisted on in the 1948 platform. His changes led to a walkout of many southern Democrats.

"There can be no hedging, no watering down. To those who say that we are rushing the issue of civil rights—I say to them, we are 172 years late."

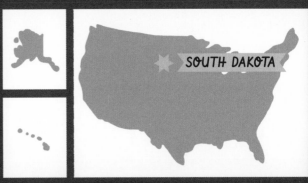

SOUTH DAKOTA

NAME: Hubert Humphrey

LED CRUSADES ON CIVIL RIGHTS WHICH RESULTED IN THE VOTING RIGHTS ACT

BORN: 1911 **DIED:** 1978

WHY? Humphrey channeled the needs of America's poor, addressed directly and unapologetically the divide in this country between races, and spent a lifetime working on legislation to help America heal on these fronts.

Humphrey spent the rest of his life fighting for this and other **PROGRESSIVE CAUSES**, becoming Vice President under Lyndon B. Johnson, and coming within a few thousand votes of winning the presidency in 1968 against Richard Nixon. All of it was within a Democratic party that has remained the home for African American struggles in the United States and paved the way for the party's 2008 nominee: Barack Obama, the first African American president of the United States.

THE TRAILBLAZE CONTINUES...

While Republicans work to deny African Americans the right to vote throughout the country, introducing voter suppression laws and other efforts, it is the Democratic party that continues to fight for civil rights. Not surprisingly, more than 90% of African Americans vote for the Democratic candidate for president each year. This is largely Hubert Humphrey's doing.

Hattie Caraway

Hattie Caraway, born in 1878, did not set out to make history as the first woman elected to a full term in the United States Senate. But that's exactly what she did!

Born in Bakerville, Tennessee and raised in nearby Hustberg, she graduated from Dickson College with a **BACHELOR OF ARTS DEGREE**—a rare level of education for a woman at that time. She married Thaddeus Caraway in 1902 and the couple had three children while Thaddeus practiced law, then climbed the ladder of American politics—Congressman, then Senator—before he died in 1931.

As was common practice, Hattie was named as **THADDEUS' SUCCESSOR** for the duration of his term. Widows often received this honor and were then expected to step aside for the real politicians once an election had taken place. But Hattie didn't see it that way.

"The time has passed when a woman should be placed in a position and kept there only while someone else is being groomed for the job."

When she was presiding over the U.S. Senate in her husband's place, Caraway announced that she would **RUN FOR THE SEAT HERSELF**. She won the Democratic primary, then the general election, **SHATTERING BARRIERS FOR WOMEN** in her wake.

MISSOURI

NAME: Hattie Caraway

POLITICAL ACTIVIST

BORN: 1878 **DIED:** 1950

WHY? Caraway was an American politician and became the first woman elected to a full U.S. Senate term.

Caraway served on a number of committees, including Commerce, Agriculture and Forestry, and Enrolled Bills, the last of which she chaired. She faced John Little McLellan in her 1938 reelection campaign, **WHO ARGUED A MAN COULD DO THE JOB BETTER**. The voters disagreed, and Caraway was **REELECTED**.

THE TRAILBLAZE CONTINUES...
A record number of women ran for Congress in 2018, continuing in the footsteps of Hattie.

Lyndon B. Johnson

Lyndon B. Johnson's career took him to the height of power and led to the kind of RADICAL CHANGE few could have imagined in areas from civil rights to the creation of MEDICARE (a government program that guaranteed health care for seniors). However, it was his GREAT SOCIETY programs that lifted millions OUT OF POVERTY and helped protect against countless others facing the grim realities of being poor.

"Until we address unequal history, we cannot overcome unequal opportunity. It must be our goal to assure that all Americans play by the same rules and all Americans play against the same odds. And if our efforts continue, and if our will is strong, and if our hearts are right, and if courage remains our constant companion, then, my fellow Americans, I am confident we shall overcome."

Born in 1908, Lyndon B. Johnson grew up in a small town in Texas Hill Country. When his father fell on hard times, Johnson saw firsthand how poverty can destroy families. Johnson enrolled at Texas State University, where he edited his college newspaper and taught at a Mexican American school to pay for his education. He became politically active, serving as a congressional aide before WINNING A SPOT IN CONGRESS himself in the 1937 election. On his second try, he won a U.S. Senate seat in 1948. He spent his legislative days working to BRING ELECTRICITY to the Hill Country where he'd grown up, finding ways to improve the lives of the least fortunate, and NEVER FORGETTING HIS ROOTS.

Part of Johnson's work during his career was designing the law for **MEDICARE**, which he signed in 1965, to both pay homage to Harry Truman's idea of guaranteeing medical care for the poor and elderly, and complete the work of Johnson's mentor, Franklin Roosevelt, who original planned a Medicare-style provision to be part of the Social Security law back in 1935. There are more than **49 MILLION** Americans covered by Medicare as a result. Johnson presented Truman and his wife with the very first two Medicare cards after signing the Medicare bill in 1965.

MICHIGAN

NAME: Lyndon B. Johnson

CHAMPIONED PROGRAMS FOR HEALTH, EDUCATION, AND CIVIL RIGHTS

BORN: 1908 **DIED:** 1973

WHY? Johnson succeeded in dislodging the southern roadblock to civil rights and became the 36th president of the United States.

Health Insurance

SOCIAL SECURITY ACT

NAME OF BENEFICIARY
Harry S. Truman

CLAIM NUMBER
488-40-6969A

SEX
M

IS ENTITLED TO
Hospital Insurance

EFFECTIVE DATE
7-1-66

Johnson rose to Senate Majority Leader, then **VICE PRESIDENT UNDER JOHN F. KENNEDY**. When Kennedy was assassinated, Johnson took office as president. Before taking office, he made it clear what he'd do when he ran for election. He would wage a war on poverty—a war that ended up cutting the number of Americans living below the poverty line from 23% to 12%. Long after he left office in 1968, Johnson remained proudest of his efforts to improve the lives of the poor, along with his work on civil rights. His final public speech, given against doctor's orders, touched on the racism and economic gap that comes from being **"BLACK IN A WHITE SOCIETY"**.

THE TRAILBLAZE CONTINUES...

Johnson's efforts on racial equality and economic security are central to the Democratic party's efforts to this day, with Obamacare in many ways modeled on Johnson's Medicare effort. Defending his social programs is what brings Americans who believe we all deserve more secure lives together, in defense of a fairer, Great Society.

David Nelson

David Nelson took on a task many believed was impossible. In Utah, one of the most conservative states in the U.S., Nelson has made it his life's work to **ADVANCE THE CAUSE OF LGBT EQUALITY** at the state and local level. Nelson is a member of the Cannon family, a prominent Utah politically connected family dating back to the nineteenth century. He entered politics while still studying political science at the University of Utah in the 1980s, serving as vice president of the Lesbian and Gay Student Union at the school. In 1985 he founded Gay Community Inc., a nonprofit dedicated to LGBT rights, and was the first-ever openly gay politician to run for Salt Lake City Council. In 1986 he moved onto the Fairness Fund, a group that eventually merged with the national Human Rights Campaign.

In every major civil rights battle waged on behalf of the LGBT community, Nelson made sure that the citizens of Utah were not left behind. Whether it was the 1993 **MARCH ON WASHINGTON** by the LGBT community or numerous legal efforts, such as the late-90s effort to **REPEAL UTAH'S LAW** against homosexual relationships, Nelson was central to making Utah **A MORE HOSPITABLE PLACE FOR EVERYONE.** In 1997 he was named to the Hate Crimes Working Group by the United States Department of Justice, which led to a national symposium with numerous Utah sponsors.

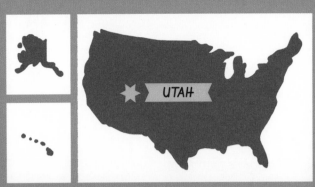

NAME: David Nelson

LGBT ACTIVIST

BORN: 1962

WHY? David's work as a legislative and executive lobbyist accomplished the adoption of several LGBT-weapon-friendly state and local laws, rules, ordinances, and policies, and the rejection of other legislation.

LOVE IS LOVE

TO CHANGE THE ELECTORAL CALCULATIONS, he founded GayVoteUtah.com to help LGBT residents of Utah register to vote. And to be sure no one ever forgot how far the community had come, he created the Utah Stonewall Hall of Fame in 2006.

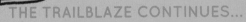

THE TRAILBLAZE CONTINUES...
the Utah Stonewall Democrats, originally created by Nelson, continue to change the political landscape in Utah, creating competitive races in the fourth congressional district and making it clear that even in Utah, there's a home for the LGBT community.

Clarina Nichols

PIONEERING NEWSPAPER EDITOR

Clarina I. H. Nichols was born in West Townshend, Vermont and saw firsthand how **WOMEN WITHOUT MONEY HAD VERY FEW OPTIONS** in nineteenth century American life. Her father was the town's "overseer of the poor", and Clarina **LISTENED TO THE CONVERSATIONS HE HAD WITH DESPERATE WOMEN IN ABUSIVE MARRIAGES** who couldn't leave or create lives of their own. These conversations inspired Clarina's passion for women's rights and she became determined to do something about them.

In 1843 Clarina left her first husband who had physically and emotionally abused her throughout their marriage. She set off to be a journalist, writing for the *Windham County Democrat*, even though her salary was a small portion of what a man would make for the same work. **SHE WROTE EDITORIALS POINTING OUT THAT WITHOUT THE ABILITY TO WORK OR LEAVE THEIR HUSBANDS, WOMEN COULDN'T BE EXPECTED TO THRIVE ON THEIR OWN.** Her editorials became a critical part of the newspaper's work, and once the paper's editor—her second husband George Nichols—became sick, she took over editing it too.

> "Though I bought the dress I'm wearing with my own money, my husband by law owns it, not of his own will, but by a law adopted by bachelors and other women's husbands."

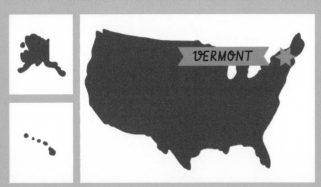

VERMONT

NAME: Clarina Nichols

PIONEERING NEWSPAPER EDITOR

BORN: 1810 DIED: 1885

WHY? Nichols was one of the first to grasp the importance of economic rights for women, and the need for wives to keep their property and wages away from their husbands' control.

In the years leading up to the Civil War, Clarina worked for progressive organizations ranging from the **NATIONAL WOMEN'S RIGHTS CONVENTION** in Worcester, to serving as a conduit on The Underground Railroad, moving her family to Kansas when the battle over whether it would be a slave or free state became violent. Her work was so significant that Susan B. Anthony picked Clarina to write her own chapter in the book, *HISTORY OF WOMEN'S SUFFRAGE*, published in 1881, four years before Clarina died.

THE TRAILBLAZE CONTINUES... Clarina's work on behalf of women's suffrage led to Kansas adopting the right of women to vote in 1912. In that same state, 78 years later, Joan Finney became the first female elected governor of Kansas, followed shortly thereafter by Kathleen Sibelius.

Mildred Loving

Mildred Loving was born in 1940, and grew up in Central Point, Virginia. Her background included several races, making her a woman of color in the South during a time when many laws discriminated on the basis of race. Loving spent a great deal of her life trying to put an end to one particular part of that discrimination: **THE RIGHT TO MARRY ANYONE OF ANY RACE**.

Her husband, Richard Loving was a white man who also grew up in Central Point. Richard and Mildred fell in love and in 1958 got **MARRIED IN WASHINGTON, D.C.** and then returned to their home in Virginia.

However, Virginia had a **LAW** against people of different races marrying that dated back to 1924. Police raided the newlywed's home and **ARRESTED THEM** for violating this law. They pleaded guilty and were sentenced to **PRISON**. However, they were given the option to avoid going to prison if they **MOVED OUT OF VIRGINIA**—the state they both considered home. The sentence meant that the Lovings would not be allowed to return to Virginia together for a period of 25 years. They would not even be allowed to travel together to visit family—regardless of the circumstance—simply because they were married.

VIRGINIA

NAME: Mildred Loving

TRAILBLAZING ACTIVIST FIGHTING TO ABOLISH LAWS BANNING INTERRACIAL MARRIAGE

BORN: 1940 **DIED:** 2008

WHY? Mildred Loving stood up for what she believed. She fought for the right to marry her husband and live in Virginia and for all couples to marry whoever they choose, regardless of their race.

They moved, but they also decided to fight the decision in court. Supported by the American Civil Liberties Union, the Lovings appealed their conviction, but lost at each level until the court case reached the U.S. Supreme Court. In 1967, though, the Supreme Court ruled in favor of the Lovings, calling marriage, "ONE OF THE BASIC CIVIL RIGHTS OF MAN", and ended any state's ability to deny a marriage certificate based on race.

"I am still not a political person, but I am proud that Richard's and my name is on a court case that can help reinforce the love, the commitment, the fairness, and the family that so many people, black or white, young or old, gay or straight seek in life. I support the freedom to marry for all. That's what Loving, and loving, are all about."

The Lovings returned to Virginia with their three children, where they lived together until Richard died in 1975. Mildred remained a resident of the state she helped change until she died in 2008.

THE TRAILBLAZE CONTINUES...
The world celebrates the aptly-named Loving Day every June 12, in honor of the brave quest by Mildred and her husband. The case also served as a useful framework for the legal effort to legalize gay marriage.

Jenny Durkan

Jenny Durkan changed what is possible for women growing up in Seattle, no matter who they love. She became the **FIRST LESBIAN MAYOR** of the city, and the first female mayor of Seattle in almost 100 years.

Durkan was born in 1958 and grew up in Issaquah, Washington, with her six siblings in a suburb of Seattle. She attended Notre Dame, before returning home to earn a law degree at the University of Washington, completing the goal that she'd had since she was five years old of becoming a lawyer.

She practiced in Seattle, working in criminal defense, and expanding her work on issues ranging from **GUN CONTROL TO MORE HUMANE TREATMENTS FOR THOSE SUFFERING FROM DRUG ADDICTION**.

In 2009, President Barack Obama named her a U.S. Attorney for Western Washington state. She pioneered a civil rights division as part of her new oversight, helped bring to justice those who plotted acts of terror and supported victims of identity theft. But when an opportunity to run for Mayor of Seattle came up in 2017, she took the chance, and the relationships she'd built throughout her career helped her win a close race. She became Mayor of Seattle where she lives today with her wife, Dana Garvey, and their two children. She's been a **FIERCE ADVOCATE OF THE PROGRESSIVE EFFORTS** in Seattle, from the $15 minimum wage law passed prior to her ascension, to a gun storage law that has survived court challenges, making Seattle safer.

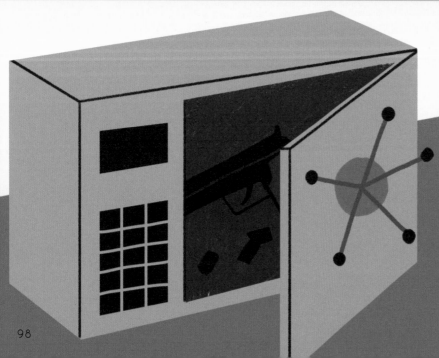

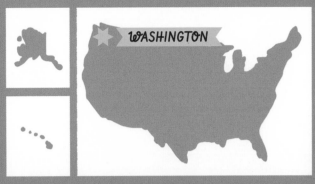

"We must remember that our common bonds, our common purposes are so much more powerful than our challenges and differences."

NAME: Jenny Durkan

POLITICIAN AND CIVIL RIGHTS ACTIVIST

BORN: 1958

WHY? Durkan was an openly gay mayor and worked for decades on behalf of poor criminal defendants. Through her pro bono work on behalf of indigent defendants, to her present-day job on behalf of the entire community of Seattle, Durkan has never stopped her efforts for those in need of help.

THE TRAILBLAZE CONTINUES... Following her election, scores of other LGBTQ+ candidates filed for office in 2018, winning races across the country, and guaranteeing that as the fight for LGBTQ+ rights continues, those affected by it will have a seat at the table.

Dale Lee

$$E = MC^2$$

Dale Lee, a lifelong West Virginia resident and **LONG-TIME TEACHER**, understood that things needed to change for teachers in his state. Lee taught special education for 22 years before taking a leave of absence to become the president of the West Virginia Education Association in 2008. He understood that small alterations to working conditions simply wouldn't be enough. Drastic measures were needed to help West Virginia's teachers experience the **BASIC QUALITY OF LIFE** necessary to do their jobs well.

Lee understood what his membership needed when they were attacked by Republicans in the state government. In the fall of 2017, Governor Jim Justice and the Republicans in the state legislature tried to renege on their commitment to the Public Employees Insurance Agency. The PEIA had guaranteed **HEALTH CARE BENEFITS** to current and former employees that included a small contribution for things like prescription drugs. The lawmakers tried to change the deal which would mean PEIA members would have to pay for 30% of the cost of the life saving drugs—hundreds and hundreds of dollars in many cases!

The money saved by sacrificing the health of public employees was to go to a tax break for businesses. When Lee and others went to the state capital to meet with legislators, they were RIDICULED by the people elected to serve the people. Governor Justice said any teachers who didn't follow him were "bunnies".

NAME: Dale Lee

HELPED LEAD THE WEST VIRGINIA TEACHERS' STRIKE OF 2018

WHY? Lee is working to increase salaries for all school employees, ensure public education funding remains a priority for our elected leaders, and increase the level of respect shown to education employees for the tremendous jobs they do.

So they took action. Wearing signature BUNNY EARS, the teachers protested. The demands were small: A PAY RAISE (West Virginia was way behind almost all other states in teacher pay) and for the state to HONOR ITS COMMITMENT to teachers on health care.

THE STRIKE WORKED! West Virginia approved a small pay raise and kept benefits for health care as they were.

"The real winners here are the students of West Virginia. Because West Virginia is now making a real investment in education."

THE TRAILBLAZE CONTINUES...The strike sparked similar action in other states, such as Oklahoma and Arizona. Democrats across the country have adopted increases in teacher pay as a key proposal.

Robert La Follette

AMERICAN LAWYER AND POLITICIAN

Robert La Follette shaped the **PROGRESSIVE MOVEMENT** from the end of the 1800s well into the 1900s, and made **WISCONSIN'S ROLE** in that movement undeniable.

La Follette's was born in 1855 in Primrose, Wisconsin. His father died when he was just eight months old, forcing him to grow up quickly—he did, **GIVING HIS FIRST PUBLIC SPEECH AT AGE THREE**, working on the family farm in Primrose, and developing an interest in politics that led him to win oratory awards and a role on the student newspaper at the University of Wisconsin. It was here that he met his wife, Belle Case, a feminist who also helped **SHAPE HIS WORLDVIEW THROUGH FEMINISM**.

By 1880, he was admitted to the Wisconsin state bar association, and held his first public office as district attorney for Dane County. He was elected to Congress in 1884 and a life in **CONVENTIONAL POLITICS** seemed like the most obvious future ahead.

"The will of the people shall be the law of the land."

However, in 1891 he was **OFFERED A BRIBE** and it opened his eyes to the **CORROSIVE ROLE OF MONEY IN POLITICS.** By the end of the century he'd become a national leader for reigning in the out-of-control action of **BIG BUSINESS** in the United States. He was elected Governor of Wisconsin in 1900 and made it his mission to make a change.

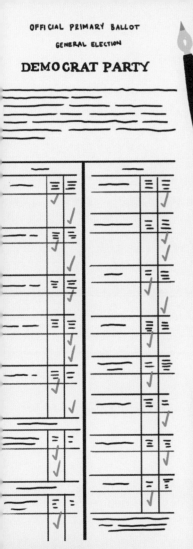

By 1903, La Follette had implemented a **PRIMARY ELECTION SYSTEM** in the state. This meant that **VOTERS** could select candidates, rather than a few power brokers who could be easily bribed to pick someone for nomination. He also changed the tax system so that railroads were paying based on the assets they owned (which were worth a lot of money) and not just their annual profits. That money went to the state to be used to improve the quality of life of Wisconsin's citizens. By 1905, he headed to the United States Senate, to advocate for these policies at the national level.

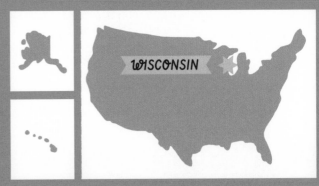

WISCONSIN

NAME: Robert La Follette

AMERICAN LAWYER AND POLITICIAN

BORN: 1855 DIED: 1925

WHY? Robert La Follette pioneered the public airing of how legislators voted to force them to reveal any untoward methods to stop progressive reforms.

"Men must be aggressive for what is right if government is to be saved from those who are aggressive for what is wrong.

The nation has awakened somewhat slowly to a realization of its peril, but it has responded with gathering momentum. The Progressive movement now has the support of all the moral forces that the solution of a great problem can command.

The outlook is hopeful. There is no room for pessimism."

He expanded his **PROGRESSIVE WORK ON BEHALF OF UNIONS**, securing passage of a bill that banned railroads from forcing workers to stay on the job for more than 16 straight hours. And he helped pass a national constitutional amendment that gave voters the chance to elect U.S. senators directly, another way to eliminate big business from buying our elected officials.

He ran for president several times, always on a progressive platform, and while he never won, he always refocused the conversation, forcing candidates to move to the left. In 1924, just before his death, he received 16.6% of the vote, **ONE OF THE BEST SHOWINGS BY A THIRD-PARTY CAMPAIGN IN U.S. HISTORY.**

THE TRAILBLAZE CONTINUES... La Follette's wife, two sons, and a grandson all remained active in Wisconsin politics. And few could miss the similarities between La Follette's campaigns and the rise of Senator Bernie Sanders in 2016.

Harriet Elizabeth Byrd

Harriet Elizabeth Byrd was born in 1926 and grew up in Wyoming which even today is not a particularly diverse state—around 92% of the population is white with just 1% of the state's population African American. But through perseverance and persuasion, Byrd proved that it is possible to **CHANGE LAWS** that discriminate and that it is even possible for an **AFRICAN AMERICAN** to be **ELECTED IN AN OVERWHELMINGLY WHITE SPACE**.

Byrd grew up in Cheyenne, the daughter of a railroad mechanic and a homemaker. Her grandfather had moved to Wyoming in 1876, so Byrd had deep roots in the state. Three years after graduating high school she married her husband James in 1947.

She went on to earn a **DEGREE IN EDUCATION** from West Virginia State in 1949. But when she returned to Laramie, Wyoming to apply for a teaching position, she was **TURNED DOWN BECAUSE OF HER RACE**.

Eventually, ten years later, she broke the color barrier, and the school reversed its position. James also broke barriers, becoming the **FIRST AFRICAN AMERICAN CHIEF OF POLICE** seven years later, in 1966.

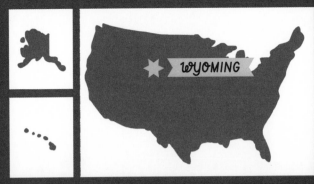

WYOMING

NAME: Harriet Elizabeth Byrd

EDUCATOR, ACTIVIST, POLITICIAN

BORN: 1926 **DIED:** 2015

WHY? Harriet Elizabeth Byrd was the first African American woman elected to the legislator in Wyoming.

After a distinguished career in education, Harriet turned to politics, and in 1980, was elected to the **WYOMING HOUSE OF REPRESENTATIVES.** Later, in 1988, she was elected **WYOMING STATE SENATOR.** She was the first African American to serve in either chamber.

Her work on a range of progressive issues changed the state. She helped establish a day honoring **MARTIN LUTHER KING, JR.,** improved safety measures required for cars, and an expansion of the safety net for those in need.

Her actions mattered. For African Americans in Wyoming, it was no longer just a dream to see someone from their world working in public service, they could now see a **WOMAN OF COLOR** doing it.

THE TRAILBLAZE CONTINUES... Harriet's son, James, was a Wyoming state representative, holding her old seat. And the University of Wyoming has a speaking series in her name.

The United States is brimming with inspirational characters—more than we can fit on the pages of this book. Here are just a few more of some of America's most amazing trailblazers. Who inspires you? Why not make your own list of 50 trailblazers from around the country?

BILLIE JEAN KING, CALIFORNIA

Born: 1943

This Grand Slam champion tennis player has worked hard on and off the court to fight against injustice and discrimination around the world. She has elevated the status of women's professional tennis, fought for women to get the same pay as men, and is a tireless activist for LGBTQ+ rights.

WALTER PHILIP REUTHER, WEST VIRGINIA

Born: 1907 Died: 1970

Reuther was the president of the United Automobile Workers and was a champion of industrial democracy and civil rights. His excellent negotiating skills helped gain annual pay raises, cost-of-living increases, unemployment benefits, health and welfare benefits, and early-retirement options for members of the UAW.

EDMUND MUSKIE, MAINE

Born: 1914 Died: 1996

Muskie was a politician who worked hard to help clean up the environment and his efforts earned him the nickname 'Mr. Clean'. He was involved in a long list of environmental legislations but two of the most noticeable were the Clean Air Act of 1970 and the Clean Water Act of 1972.

RUTH BADER GINSBURG, NEW YORK

Born: 1933

The second female justice of the U.S. Supreme Court, Ginsburg has spent much of her career fighting hard for gender equality and women's rights. She has received countless awards for her work along with honorary PhDs and a spot on the *Forbes* magazine's 100 Most Powerful Women. And she's not finished yet! Aged 86, Ginsburg continues to serve on the High Court.

EDWARD R. MURROW, WASHINGTON

Born: 1908 Died: 1965

Murrow was a radio and television broadcaster and was a key figure during the formative years of American broadcast journalism. He gained fame and recognition during World War II for his honest and incisive reports.

JOHN TRUDELL, NEBRASKA

Born: 1946 Died: 2015

Poet, musician, actor, and activist. John Trudell has a long list of achievements under his belt. He was a spokesperson for the Native American rights movement and was heavily involved in working for indigenous human rights.

CHERYL REEVE, NEW JERSEY

Born: 1966

Two-time winner of the WNBA Coach of the Year award, Reeve has won the most games of any female coach. She is a tireless activist and uses her platform to fight for the rights of women, fair coverage of women's sports, equal opportunity for young women in sports, and LGBTQ+ issues.

BEATRICE "BEA" ROSE, ALASKA

Born: 1921 Died: 2007

Bea Rose was an incredible educator and community activist. Some of her many achievements include creating and sustaining the first Jewish synagogue in Anchorage, working as a speech therapist for students with disabilities, advocating to improve mental health resources, and fighting for women's rights.

ELIZABETH WARREN, OKLAHOMA

Born: 1949

Politician and academic, Warren has used her position to fight against the injustice of a country where the rich are getting richer and the poor are getting poorer. She has a long list of achievements, one of which saw her creating the Consumer Financial Protection Bureau which protects people from financial tricks and traps.

PAUL WELLSTONE, MINNESOTA

Born: 1944 Died: 2002

College professor turned politician Wellstone was a leader of the progressive wing of the national Democratic Party. He's quoted as saying, "I don't represent the big oil companies, the big pharmaceuticals, or the big insurance industry. They already have great representation in Washington. It's the rest of the people that need representation."

STACEY ABRAMS, GEORGIA

Born: 1973

Novelist, lawyer, and politician, Abrams is a member of the Democratic Party and was the first female African American to deliver a State of Union response in 2019. One of her most influential pieces of work is her Fair Fight Action. She launched this after the mismanagement of the 2018 elections, to ensure that every Georgian has a voice in the electoral system.

DAVID HOGG, FLORIDA

Born: 2000

David Hogg is a survivor of the 2018 Stoneman Douglas High School shooting. Since then he has become an advocate for gun control, worked hard to fight against gun violence, and led and participated in numerous protests, marches, and boycotts in connection with gun control. He is a founding member of "Never Again MSD."

SUSAN B. ANTHONY, MASSACHUSETTS

Born: 1820 Died: 1906

Susan B. Anthony was an advocate for women's rights and was a founder of the National Women's Suffrage Association in 1869. She was instrumental in securing the vote for women and traveled around the country with her fellow suffragette, Elizabeth Cady Stanton, delivering speeches in favor of women's rights.

LESLI FOSTER, COLORADO

Born: 1975

Foster is an Emmy award-winning journalist who has reported on hard-hitting stories across the country such as the aftermath of 9/11 and the 40th anniversary of the March on Washington. Foster has had the opportunity to cover major events, but her focus is on working with ordinary people who use their lives to do extraordinary things.

JOSEFINA FRANCO, ARIZONA

Born: 1897 Died: 1972

Franco dedicated her life to civil rights and helping disadvantaged people. Among her many accomplishments, she helped build bridges between the English and Spanish communities in Phoenix and set up the newspaper *El Sol* which spoke out against racism, discrimination, and injustices of Mexican Americans.

HANNAH BROWN, NEVADA

Born: 1939

Brown has spent her life battling for race and gender equality. As one of 15 African American kids in school, she has worked hard to break barriers and overcome obstacles becoming the president of the Las Vegas Urban Chamber of Commerce. She's won numerous awards, including Most Promising Black Women in Corporate America.

Index

Glossary

ACCOUNTABILITY Being responsible.

ACTIVIST Someone who campaigns to bring about social or political change.

ADVOCATES Publicly supports something.

AMASS Gather together.

ARRAY A good range.

ASPIRING Hoping to become.

BARRIOS Town districts.

BESEECHINGLY Pleading urgently.

BLACKBALLED Rejected or banned.

BOYCOTT Refuse to take part in something as a protest.

CATALYST Someone who causes great change.

CIVIL RIGHTS The rights of people to political and social freedom and equality.

COALITION Partnership.

CONCEDE Allow.

CONSERVATIVE Traditional, not liking change.

CONTAGIOUS Likely to spread to others.

DECADES Periods of ten years.

DECIMATION The killing of a large number of creatures.

DENIGRATION Unfair criticism of someone.

DILIGENTLY Carefully.

DISCRIMINATION The unjust treatment of a particular group of people.

EASEMENT The right to use someone else's land.

ELOQUENTLY With a clear, strong message.

EMPATHY Understanding and sharing other people's feelings.

ELEVATED Increased in importance.

FASCISM A political system with a leader who is a dictator.

FEMINISM The belief that women should have equal rights to men.

GRASSROOTS Ordinary people in society or an organization.

HONORARY DOCTORATE A university degree given to someone who is not a student but has achieved something important.

HUNTINGTON'S DISEASE A disease that damages nerve cells in the brain, causing mental health problems and coordination difficulties.

ICON Someone seen as an important symbol.

IMPOSED Forced.

INAUGURATION Ceremony to mark a new president.

INCARCERATED Imprisoned.

INDIGENOUS Native.

LEAVENING Changing for the better.

LEGACY Something that continues from history.

LIBERAL Open to accepting different ideas or opinions.

MEAGRE Limited.

MOMENTUM Force gained by something moving.

MORATORIUM A stopping of something for a limited amount of time.

ORATORY Skillful public speaking.

PARKINSON'S DISEASE A disease of the nervous system, causing shaking and movement difficulties.

PAROLE The release of a prisoner on condition of their good behavior.

PERCEIVE Realize.

PIONEERING Using new ideas or methods.

POLIO A disease that can cause paralysis of the body.

PRAIRIE A large, flat, open area of grassland.

PROBATION Someone being supervised after their release from prison.

PROSPERITY Good fortune, being successful.

RADICAL Huge change.

REPEAL Remove a law.

RESOLVE Firm decision to act.

REVERENCE Deep respect or admiration.

RHETORICAL Written or spoken conversation for effect.

SAVVY Knowledgeable.

SEGREGATION Keeping one group of people separate from everyone else.

SENATE Group of politicians who make laws.

SYMPOSIUM A meeting.

UNANIMOUS Everyone in agreement.

UNPRECEDENTED Never seen or known before.

VARSITY Sport event or team relating to a university.

Further reading

I SPY THE 50 STATES
Author: Sharyn Rosart
Illustrator: Sol Linero

Take a tour around the 50 states of the USA, from Maine to Hawaii, peeking through the holes as you go. Colorfully illustrated board book with images depicting the people, landmarks, and things that make each state unique, as well as one item that it has "in common" with the state next door. Can you "spy" it is through the hole?

THE 50 STATES
Author: Gabrielle Balkan
Illustrator: Sol Linero

Ghost towns, swamp tours, the center of the universe... bacon donuts, brainy berries, salmon jerky... The French Fry King, The Mother of Oregon, The Queen of Blues... be inspired by the inventiveness, beauty and diversity of the United States in this curious collection of fact-filled maps.

THE 50 STATES ACTIVITY BOOK
Author: Gabrielle Balkan
Illustrator: Sol Linero

Pack your bags and take the journey of a lifetime with this fun-filled activity book packed with maps, wildlife, people, and places unique to America's 50 states. Enjoy state trivia, picture scrambles, dot-to-dots, plus a double-sided fold-out map and more than 50 stickers included in this activity book like no other!

50 CITIES OF THE U.S.A.
Author: Gabrielle Balkan
Illustrator: Sol Linero

Explore skyscraper streets, museum miles, local food trucks, and city parks of the United States of America and discover more than 2,000 facts that celebrate the people, culture, and diversity that have helped make America what it is today. From Anchorage to Washington D.C., take a trip through America's well-loved cities with this unique A-Z like no other, lavishly illustrated and annotated with key cultural icons, from famous people and inventions to events, food, and monuments.

THE 50 STATES FUN FACTS
Author: Gabrielle Balkan
Illustrator: Sol Linero

Take an incredible journey with this activity book packed with everything that makes America's 50 states unique. Celebrate the people, places, and food of the U.S.A in an activity book like no other! From Animals and Things that Go to People and Places and Festivals and Cultural events, this is a fact-filled celebration of the United States of America, which includes a make-your-own puzzle of the 50 states on the final spread.